HEALEY

Dedication

To Margot, Cecilia and Kate for their encouragement, help and patience.

HEALEY
The Specials

GEOFFREY HEALEY

GENTRY BOOKS
LONDON

First published 1980
ISBN 0 85614 062 7

Published by Gentry Books Limited,
15 Pont Street, London SW1.
Distributed in the USA by

Osceola, Wisconsin 54020, USA

Filmset by Tradespools Limited, Frome.
Printed and bound in Great Britain by
Butler & Tanner Limited, Frome.

Contents

Acknowledgements *7*
Beginnings *11*
The First Healeys *24*
The Nash Healey Specials *47*
After the Show: The First Twenty *60*
The Special Test Cars *74*
The First Record Breakers *87*
The Cars of 1954 *95*
200 mph *110*
The 100 S *122*
Into the Glorious Sixties *146*
SR and XR 37 *172*
At the End: A New Beginning *187*
Appendix *195*
Index *199*

Acknowledgements

The author gratefully acknowledges the following for their kind permission to reproduce photographs and extracts: *Autosport*, B.L. Cars Ltd., Edward Eves, Guy Griffiths, Kate Healey, Robert Roskrow and *Road and Track*.

He would also like to point out that it has not been possible to trace the source of all photographs, and wishes to apologise to anyone who is not included in this list.

Introduction

With my two books, *Austin Healey* and *More Healeys*, I gave a general account of the Big Healeys and their small brothers, the Sprites and Midgets. The response from enthusiasts has been overwhelming, resulting in a steady bombardment of letters, many of which I have been unable to answer. I have received telephone calls from all corners of the earth, at all hours of the day and night, while many enthusiasts have brought their beautifully restored models to Barford. All these letters, phone calls and visits were prompted by a desire for more information about Healeys, both the cars and the people, and high on the list were queries about the special cars.

Whereas my first two books concentrated on the production cars, in this new book I have paid more attention to the special cars, including the 100 S, now the most sought-after of Austin Healey models. A conversation about the new book with one of my friends from Detroit brought the rejoinder, 'Specials? All your cars are special.' He went on to point out how Ford's prototype build of a new model was equivalent to some of our production runs. Their engineering and prototype facilities certainly are enormous when compared to the small resources at our disposal for the construction of our cars.

DMH and I have enjoyed visits to club centres all over the world, to California, Oregon, Kentucky, Australia, Hawaii, Germany, and of course throughout Britain. The opportunity to examine and try many of our old products certainly stimulates the phagocytes and makes one eager to try to make a new car. I have therefore taken this opportunity to bring the Healey story up to date, with details of the developments over recent years, following those happy days of yore.

Early in 1980, Ivy, the wife of DMH and mother of Bic, John and myself, died peacefully. Over the years, she was always there in the background, sustaining the family on what small amount of income was left after the design, development and construction of motor cars had taken the lion's share. She hoarded and preserved vast quantities of photographs and kept diaries and all the letters we had written home. This material has been invaluable in the preparation of the true Healey story.

Despite my attempts to provide a factual background to this story, many of my writings have been distorted to provide a few more myths, and I trust that this new book will finally put to rest a few of the more extravagant ones.

The golden wedding party for DMH and Ivy and all the family, in October 1971. (Robert Roskrow)

Beginnings

The Healey family comes from Cornwall, the extreme south-west of England. The family home is at Perranporth, on the north coast, where a beach 3 miles long lies exposed to the full force of the Atlantic Ocean. Due west is the USA, a country to which many Cornish people emigrated in the past, to seek work as engineers on the railroads and in the mines.

Cornwall has had a strong association with engineering and produced some fine engineers, including Richard Trevithick, who was responsible for the world's first locomotive. Remote from the industrial centres of England, and badly served by transport, the Cornish people needed to establish their own foundries and engineering shops, to support the tin and copper mines that played such a crucial part in the economy. With the decline of the mining industry, the demand on local engineering facilities diminished, and many Cornish engineers were forced to emigrate to the colonies and the USA. My father-in-law, who was born and bred a Newfoundlander, felt he had returned home when he retired to Cornwall, for he found the life style and the spoken word to be almost identical.

An excellent picture of the old Cornwall was given in the BBC's series 'Poldark'. Winston Graham, the author, spent much of his life in Perranporth and drew inspiration from the tales the local inhabitants love to

The red and black coupé with Perranporth beach in the background.

narrate. Many of the characters and stories portrayed in 'Poldark' are familiar to people who lived in the old Perranporth.

It was into this very individual environment that my father, Donald Mitchell Healey, was born on 3rd July 1898. Amongst the vast stores of material in the family archives, I managed to unearth an autobiography which he had started to write. Unfortunately, he found time to write only two chapters, and these follow.

Getting the Taste

My earliest memories of a motor car are of my father starting his Panhard Levassor and of one occasion in particular when he broke his arm in the attempt.

I spent my early childhood in that lovely and then unspoilt village of Perranporth on the north coast of Cornwall, where motor cars were very strange things. England was another country across the Tamar, and many miles away.

Father had bought his Panhard in London and driven it to Cornwall – a 'London to Lands End' that took three days and was probably a harder reliability trial than any I ever competed in. It was a wonderful machine: four cylinders, four speeds, drip feed lubricators and, of course, chain drive. Starting was a tedious job with the hot tubes but later a magneto was fitted which, with the help of ether injections through the compression taps, made starting easier although still with a great risk to one's limbs. I have seen one of its backfires throw a man over the bonnet! On long journeys we always carried a spare big-end bearing and it was often fitted on the road: lubrication was not very reliable! Brakes were the cause of much excitement and anxiety as they were fitted on the chain countershaft, so a broken chain meant no brakes whatsoever more than once. I have clung to my father while he hurtled down a steep Cornish hill with no brakes and no engine compression to help. But he was a born driver who had graduated from years of cycling, and I never remember him running out of road.

My first taste of real motoring came in 1909 when I made my first venture into that foreign land – England. I went to London by train to stay with my father's great friend, C A Keall, who was to drive me back to Cornwall in his new 30 hp Beeston Humber, a beautifully made car with a large tonneau body and a door in the back to give access to the rear seat. We started our journey at daybreak, and how proud I felt perched in the back of this large machine wearing goggles and a dust-coat! There was no Great West Road then except through Hounslow and Brentford to Staines, and then macadam roads and dust across the plain to Salisbury. Towards midday it got very hot and the tyres began to give trouble. Needless to say, we carried two Stepney rims and two spare covers – and used them all before we reached Cornwall. I vividly remember

DMH as a young pilot in the First World War. He said he saw no future for aeroplanes other than as machines of war, and so he joined the motor industry.

seeing England's first filling-station, run by the AA and situated between Yarcombe and Honiton with no petrol pumps but plenty of petrol in cans. Our exertions with the tyres had tired us out and we stopped for the night at Exeter. For the remainder of our journey the road to Perranporth was very narrow and the hills very steep but, fortunately, the Humber had plenty of power and surprisingly good brakes. It had a maximum speed of about 50 mph which we rarely achieved as we doubted the tyres. What a thrill it was going down the last steep hill into Perranporth, having done a journey of 260 miles in two days, black with dust and the envy of all the boys in the village!

60 mph was indeed a magic speed in those days and only reached by very powerful and expensive machines. Two friends of Father came from London in 1912 with a Prince Henry Vauxhall and an Austro-Daimler, two of the finest sports cars of the time. I rode in both these cars at over 60 mph on the then only straight road in Cornwall, on the Bodmin Moor.

My early enthusiasm for things mechanical, particularly the internal-combustion engine, coincided with the birth of the aeroplane: and this new idea soon captured my imagination. I went 300 miles to see Bleriot and his machine, and then pestered Father to let me make flying my career. He eventually agreed and allowed me to leave school

14

at a far too early age in order to become an articled pupil with the Sopwith Aviation Company, Kingston-on-Thames. In spite of paying a large premium, it meant working ten hours a day for only six shillings a week. But how lucky I was to be one of the first boys to be a pupil in the aircraft industry with the chance to learn to fly as part of my training. My early days at Sopwith's took me to their aerodrome at Brooklands where I had many flights with my hero, Harry Hawker, Sopwith's test-pilot. I shall always remember him as the finest aviator ever born and shall never forget those superb flying demonstrations he made, including flying under the Byfleet Bridge at Brooklands. Harry owned a beautiful Gregoire motor car which he often let me drive on the track although I was far too young to have a driving licence. In spite of my love of aeroplanes, I was always thrilled by those wonderful Brooklands motor race meetings held before the 1914 War.

With the advent of war, Sopwith's became our foremost aircraft producer and, under the able management of Freddy Sigrist, turned out that wonderful range of flight machines that enabled us to beat the Fokker. And may I here digress to remind readers that it was Sopwith and Sigrist who, in 1938–9, produced the Hawker Hurricane before they were even ordered by the Air Ministry, and whose foresight saved us in the Battle of Britain.

Although our work was of such national importance, I could not stand the frequent white feather presentations and, after attending one of Horatio Bottomley's meetings at the Karsino, I next day went to the recruiting office at Scotland Yard to volunteer for the Flying Corps early in 1915. I was turned down as I was then only 16 but, a few months later, I went to Shepherds Bush, put my age on two years and was accepted.

This book is concerned with motoring, and suffice it to say that I got my wings, had an argument with our own 'Archies' in France, was invalided in 1917 and posted to the Aeronautical Inspection Department – this cured my craze for aeroplanes! Beyond driving a Crossley tender in the RFC and having the use of a 4 hp Douglas and sidecar in the AID, I had little to do with motoring during those war years.

The Hard Way
or
The Oily-fingered Cornish Boy

My health not being too good as a result of my war experience, I decided to return to my native village. Internal combustion engines were still my love and I opened a garage in Perranporth in 1919 and, for three years, saw motor cars chiefly from a garage pit. This earned the title bestowed on me a few years ago in a daily paper, following a success on a Healey car – 'the oily-fingered Cornish boy'.

Just after the war, when English cars were very difficult to obtain, Father bought an American RMC (Royal Motor Company) car. Although practically unknown in this country, this was quite a sports car. It had an underslung front as well as rear axle; a 20 hp engine and a light four-seater body. Although I did not compete in this car, it was my first experience of a car with a low CG and was the commencement of my education in what road-holding meant.

In 1922 we formed the Truro and District Motor Club and held our first hill climb near Truro on a public road – at that time the police shut their eyes to such things! I had just acquired a new Buick (valve in head), six-cylinder, 30 hp and, after renovating the wings and windscreen, made fastest time of the day; and the little bronze medal with TDMC FTD was my first motoring prize.

The 'bug' having got me, I had to have a sports car and acquired an ABC, a post-war car of very advanced design powered by a 10 hp air-cooled, horizontally opposed twin engine. It was considerably lighter than its contemporaries and had a good performance, although rather unreliable. A few weeks later, I made FTD in speed trials held by the TDMC on a fairly straight mile of main road near Perranporth. My average for the flying quarter-mile was just under 66 mph.

As I lived in Cornwall, the one trial that captured my imagination was the London–Land's End and, in 1923, I started from Slough on the classic event. All went well until Porlock where I over-revved the engine and a pushrod jumped out, cutting out one cylinder; the engine eventually seized and I had to retire. I had had my first lesson!

Perranporth was situated off the main road to Land's End and my local pride made me very anxious to have the Trial pass through the village, so I set about finding a hill

DMH on a ralley with a Riley with a large Union Jack on its side. He often wore a striped blazer on rallies.

which would make it necessary for competitors to come that way. I had just acquired a new Ariel 10 hp, four-cylinder car which I had fitted with the latest Avon balloon tyres; the first real low-pressure tyres I had tried. One day, when I was following a rough road to a mine on the coast in order to test the tyres on such a surface, I found a disused road leading from the mine to St Agnes, which had a very acute hairpin on a fairly steep gradient – I had found my hill and the MCC Committee diverted the route to include the now famous Blue Hills Mine Hill for the first time in 1924. That year I was introduced to that great sportsman, Victor Riley, who, 20 years later, was to prove such a true friend. I bought a new model, a 10.8 hp Riley known as the 'Red Winger', to drive in that year's event. It was a light two-seater polished aluminium body on the well-known 10.8 side-valve engined chassis with scarlet wings. I set off for Slough for the start of the London–Land's End at Easter when, only 40 miles from Perranporth, travelling at over 60 mph, this beautiful new car burst into flames and was completely

17

destroyed. The fire was caused by a leaking petrol tank, situated over the engine, dripping petrol on to the magneto. I rushed back to Perranporth and grabbed my discarded ABC, which performed faultlessly, and won my first MCC gold medal.

Later in the year, the MCC held their longest trial: the Land's End–John-O'-Groats. Driving the new Ariel Ten with Father as co-driver, I secured a premier award. I was very impressed with the economy of this car, which was fitted with a 10 hp Swift engine, and, in conjunction with the manufacturers, arranged for an RAC officially-observed trial from Land's End to John-O'-Groats and back. Accompanied by an RAC observer, I left Land's End in September 1924. All refuelling was done by the RAC observer, the tank being filled from stamped copper measures. The set average speed was 20 mph and I was able to maintain this by driving on a weak carburettor spot at about 40 mph. This resulted in remarkable economy and the 1,500 miles was covered at an average consumption of 51 mpg. The run included ascents of Porlock and Blue Hills Mine to prove that an economy setting was not used and the result was a great tribute to the efficiency of a fine little car which, unfortunately, went out of production the following year. It was made by the manufacturers of the famous Ariel motorcycle.

My first introduction to the Triumph Company was the purchase of a 1924 Triumph 10: a beautifully made chassis fitted with an engine designed by Ricardo with his patented head and masked valves. It also had a very clever four-speed gearbox with a special interlock device to prevent gear crashing. It had a very pretty two-seater polished aluminium body but was too heavy and under-powered for trials work and, after a few runs on local test hills, I disposed of it.

The power of the Ariel was improved by the fitting of dual carburettors and, in Easter 1925, it performed well in the London–Land's End and won me a gold medal.

At the Motor Show in 1925, Fiat introduced a full four-seater car fitted with an overhead camshaft, 990 cc engine, designated the Fiat Seven. With a Rolls-Royce style of radiator and its very up-to-date specification, including four-wheel brakes, it created a sensation. The manufacturers were very keen to show that this car had the performance to match its appearance and loaned me one for the 1926 Land's End. It really did perform well, the little engine revving up to 5,000 rpm without any fuss. It ran faultlessly throughout the trial and gained me a gold medal.

Career

1914–1915	Pupil with Sopwith Aviation Co	– learning to fly with Harry Hawker.
1915–1917	Royal flying Corps	– advanced age to get accepted on flying experience – posted to unit with no aeroplanes.
		Promoted to Corporal owing to ability to drive motor cycle – on first journey drove into ditch with CO of Squadron in sidecar.
		Took RFC Wings in 1916.
		Six months on Home Defence Yorkshire (anti-Zeppelin).

	Posted overseas night bombing 1917 – invalided out of service following flying crash 1917.
1917–1919	Transferred to Aeronautical Inspectors' Department.
1920–1930	Operated own business in Cornwall and did free-lance driving for ABC, Ariel, Triumph, Riley, Invicta.
1930–1934	The successful Invicta years.
1934–1939	In charge of design and experimental work at Triumph Company – responsible for design of Gloria and Dolomite cars. Became Technical Director, Triumph Co.
1940–1944	Air Ministry work – Hobson Carburettors – Humber armoured car development – RAFVR Squadron Leader in charge Warwickshire ATC.
1944 to date	The Healey car.

Other Events

Year	Event	Car	Highlights
1925	JCC High Speed Trial – Brooklands	Ariel 10	First time on Brooklands – won gold medal.
1925	Land's End–John-O'-Groats. Land's End RAC observed trial.	Ariel 10	Measured petrol consumption 52 mpg.
1931	International 10,000 kilometre Trial	Riley 2-litre	The longest trial ever organized – traversed 37 countries in a fortnight – finished in Berlin – did my first broadcast there – won first award without loss of single mark.
1931	Paris-Nice	Riley Nine	First in class.
1931	La Turbie Hill Climb	Riley Nine	First in class.
1932	Klausen Hill Climb	Invicta	Second in unlimited class.
1932	Tourist Trophy Race	Invicta	Seized axle in practice.
1932	Brighton Speed Trials	Invicta	Tied for fastest time in class with Kay Petre who borrowed and drove same car.
1932	Paris–Nice	Invicta	Won class.

Reliability Trials

Year	Event	Car	Highlights
1923	London–Land's End	ABC	My first event, over keen to do speed on Porlock Hill, over revved engine and wrecked valve gear – a first lesson.
1924	London–Land's End	Riley 11.9 hp ABC	At 60 mph caught fire and completely destroyed – self and passenger leapt out before car had stopped. This happened 40 miles from home in Cornwall, hired car and returned home, collected old ABC, changed entry and won first gold medal. This year I discovered and introduced famous Bluehills Mine Hill to MCC.
1924	Land's End–John-O'-Groats	Ariel 10	Gold medal.
1925	London–Land's End	Ariel 10	Gold medal.
1926	London–Land's End	Fiat 7	First time car had been used in England – gold medal.
1927	London–Land's End	Rover 10	Gold medal.
1928	London–Land's End	Triumph 7	Silver medal.
1929	London–Land's End	Triumph 7 super-charged	Gold medal.
1930	London–Land's End	Fiat 10	Gold medal.

Mille Miglia

Year	Car	Highlights and Results
1948	Healey Roadster	First time in this great event – wonderful hospitality extended by Conte and Contessa Maggi at Calino. Hit large dog at 75 mph, burst tyre and broke wheel – damaged lighting and had to do last 50 miles of Autostrada with no lights at over 100 mph following an Italian car. Finished ninth in general classification – first British car. Lurani on Healey Saloon won closed car class. Won Mille Miglia medal. Elected member of Mille Miglia Club.
1949	Healey Saloon	Trouble-free run – finished fourth in touring category. T H Wisdom and G C Healey won touring category on Healey Roadster. Won Mille Miglia medal.

1950	Nash-Healey	Pushed into ditch by lorry in Apennines – pulled out by monks but finished too late to qualify.
1951	Nash-Healey	Trouble-free run but road very dangerous due to wet and traffic – finished in General Classification. Won Mille Miglia medal.
1952	Nash-Healey Saloon	Burst tyre approaching bridge, hit parapet of bridge and wrecked car.

A Triumph Dolomite roadster photographed by DMH in front of our home in Leamington Spa. At that time he was the technical director of Triumph. The American influence shows in the distinctive radiator grille.

Alpine Trials

Year	Description	Car	Highlights
1930	Austrian	Invicta	Drove Invicta on which Violet Cordey did 30,000 miles in 30,000 minutes at Brooklands and won Dewar Trophy – made fastest time on Arlberg Hill Climb beating famous German driver, Count Von Bitzy (Austro Daimler) – won Alpine Cup – awarded a free flight over Alps in Graf Zeppelin.
1930	International Alfold Alpine Trial	Invicta	Same Invicta – won Alpine Cup.
1931	International Alpine Trial	Invicta	Made fastest time on Galibier Hill Climb and won Alpine Cup.
1932	International Alpine Trial	Invicta	Made fastest time and broke Sports Car Record for Stelvio Pass Hill Climb (57 hairpins) won Alpine Cup.
1933	International Alpine Trial	Riley	Drove a 'Brooklands' Riley – baulked by foreign car on Galibier and lost first mark ever in an Alpine – finished second in class.
1934	International Alpine Trial	Triumph 10	Made fastest time in Class in Stelvio Pass Hill Climb – won Alpine Cup.
1936	International Alpine Trial	Triumph 14	Won Alpine Cup.
1948	International Rallye des Alpes	Healey Roadster	Had to stop to help injured driver – lost marks thereby and finished second.
1949	International Rallye des Alpes	Healey Silverstone	Held up at railway crossing and lost one mark – again finished second.

Rallies

Year	Rally	Car	Highlights
1928	Bournemouth	Triumph 7	Won premier award starting from John-O'-Groats.
1929	Brighton	Triumph 7	Won premier award starting from John-O'-Groats.
1929	Riga–Barcelona	Triumph 7	Won class and best British car.
1929	Monte Carlo Starting from Riga.	Triumph 7	Snowed up at Deutsches Krone (Germany) en route to Riga – had to return to Berlin and start there. Bad snow conditions, arrived two minutes outside time limit at Monte Carlo. Won class in Mont des Mules Hill Climb.

1930	Monte Carlo Starting from Tallin. Co-drivers: L Pearce and brother H Healey.	Triumph 7	1,000 miles of snow and ice to Russian border – Tallin in Esthonia – through Latvia – Lithuania – Poland – Germany. Finished seventh in whole event – first British car.
1931	Monte Carlo Starting from Stavanger.	Invicta	Crashed into telegraph pole in Sweden, knocked rear axle back – had to saw through brake rod. Finished rally on three brakes and axle out of line. Rally decided on acceleration and brake test – made best time and won rally.
1932	Monte Carlo Starting from Umea. Co-driver: Montgomery.	Invicta	Snow and ice all the way to Paris – second in rally – first British car.
1933	Monte Carlo Starting from Tallin. Co-driver: Montgomery.	Invicta	40° below zero at start – pulled the late Alan Good (Lagonda) out of ditch in Latvia – went off road to avoid runaway horse sledge in Poland – hit tree and wrecked car.
1934	Monte Carlo Starting from Athens. Co-driver: T H Wisdom.	Triumph 10	Mud conditions from Athens to Salonika, escorted by soldiers across Sidrokastren Desert. Flooded Danube at Sofia, had to be ferried across – terrible fog in Bulgaria and Hungary – snow all through Germany. Second in Rally – first British car winning outright trophy for best performance for three years.
1935	Monte Carlo Starting from Umea. Co-driver: L Pearce.	Triumph Dolomite 8-cyl	Snow all way to Denmark – following S C H Davis through fog – hit train on unguarded crossing in Denmark at 45 mph, car wrecked but passenger, Louis Pearce, and self unhurt.
1936	Monte Carlo Starting from Tallin. Co-driver: L Pearce.	Triumph Dolomite 8-cyl	800 miles of snow and ice – following a foreign competitor through Kaunas (Lithuania), saw him hit train at level crossing with fatal results – eighth place in rally – first British car.
1937	Monte Carlo Starting from Palermo (Sicily) co-drivers: T H Wisdom and Norman Black.	Triumph 12	Bad road conditions but very hot in straits of Messina – had so much time in hand able to bathe. Had engine trouble and retired at Munich.

The First Healeys

During the Second World War, DMH worked with Humber on armoured fighting vehicle development. Towards the end, when victory was in sight, his thoughts naturally turned to cars for the future. Humber were not very advanced in their thinking and DMH became increasingly frustrated with wooden-headed designers and ignorant and stubborn draughtsmen. He decided, instead, to make his own motor car. At Humber he had two brilliant colleagues, Ben Bowden the body engineer and A C (Sammy) Sampietro the chassis engineer. In their spare time these three schemed and detailed the Healey car. Contrary to certain scurrilous reports, all this work was done at home, Ben laying out the full-size body lines on the wall of his living room. Sammy was one of the most original thinkers of the day, and certainly not hide-bound by traditional constraints. Some would criticize him for not always getting the decimal point in the right place in his calculations. Unabashed, Sammy would laugh and expostulate, 'Why worry? It's only an insignificant dot and the development engineers will get it right!'

In March 1945 DMH obtained permission from the Board of Trade to proceed with the building of a prototype chassis. He also obtained the lease of a 10,000 square foot workshop at Benfords in Warwick, then occupied by the Ministry of Aircraft Production. To begin the construction of the new car, he was able to persuade Roger Menadue to leave Armstrong Whitley and join him at Warwick. Roger was to play a crucial role in the development and preparation of nearly all the Healey cars, running the

24

experimental workshop at Warwick until the end of the production of the 3000. He had come up the traditional route, starting with a long apprenticeship and garage work, followed by some years working for DMH in the experimental department at Triumph. During the war years, he worked on the manufacture of heavy bombers at Armstrong Whitley, learning much that was to prove useful to us in the construction of future prototypes and specials at Warwick.

In July 1945, DMH wrote an article that was intended to create interest in a new sports car and help sell the idea of the new Healey. This article is reproduced below:

The Enthusiast's Car
by Donald Healey

The first requisite of an enthusiast's, or 'sports' car as it is commonly termed, is 'performance' in its broadest meaning: ie it must be a vehicle capable of covering the ground over the roads it is meant to be used on, better, considerably better, than the usual vehicles, and give a good deal of pleasure to its driver whilst doing so.

I believe we should limit ourselves to 'roads' otherwise a jeep, a crawler tractor, a bull-dozer, or a buffalo may be considered to have a better performance, each in its own special sphere, although none could be described as a 'sports car'.

For immediate consideration, we can limit ourselves to a car propelled by an internal combustion engine, transmitting its power through suitable clutch, gears, etc.

The requisites of a sports car are:

A: It must be much more readily controllable than the usual car by a reasonably expert driver, even if to obtain this may mean that a novice will find the car 'difficult'.

B: It must have a high cruising speed, and enough power in reserve at such a speed to have an acceleration of the order of 5ft per sec. This requires an engine which gives plenty of power where required, and which is suitably geared. Top gear performance at 10 mph is not an essential.

In order to satisfy requirement A the various components of the car must be maintained in their proper position and alignment, under all conditions. We all know how badly a car that has been 'bent' in a crash and not straightened out properly behaves, and it is not difficult to imagine what happens when a frame weaves, twists and bends at high speed, or when springs and radius arms deform and allow the wheels to take up whatever position they like.

The most important single component of a car, and especially of a fast car, is the main frame. Unless this is really rigid in all directions, it is not much use trying to design suitable springing and steering, for the model will be vicious and 'pile up' only too often.

Most people appreciate by now that a frame must be rigid in bending in a vertical plane: doors that do not shut, or fly open when hitting a bump, are a far too visible symptom to be ignored by even the most obstinate draughtsman, although these gentlemen are very hard to convince.

25

Many understand why a frame must be torsionally rigid, but very few know how rigid a frame should be in a horizontal plane. Yet it is easy to see that centrifugal force acting at the centre of gravity tends to bend the frame like a bow, bringing the inner wheels together, and causing perhaps the worst condition of increasing over-steer. A number of well known drivers came to grief because of this: it was a marked fault of a number of Grand Prix cars up to about 1934 and of the first version of a famous town car dressed up in sporting guise.

I would put a correct, quick and sensitive steering as the second requisite. Steering connections must be rigid: flimsy steering arms, bent track or push and pull rods, and badly supported boxes have no business in a fast car. Some designers mask faults of steering geometry by introducing springiness or sponginess in the connections, but such people can never have had any experience of fast driving.

The steering geometry must be such that a slight under-steer is present. However, let us remember that in order to have a side thrust we have to turn the wheels a fraction; the tyres will deform like a spring, and tend to 'straighten back', so we must be careful not to have too much under-steer. Actually, about the best compromise is to have a slight over-steer at low speeds and large locks, and a slight under-steer at high speeds and small locks.

What must on all accounts be avoided is the reverse: a car that over-steers at high speeds is tiring to its driver, and dangerous. A number of such cars have been produced and will probably continue to be produced – not all of them across the Atlantic, either. When discussing steering, the rear wheels must be remembered. A badly located back axle, or an indifferent rear independent suspension will spoil the best steering.

Springing and wheel location are so bound up with steering that it is impossible to discuss one without the other. The amount of control we can exert through a wheel is limited to the tangential force that the said wheel can exert, ie the product of the coefficient of friction between tyre and ground and the load supported by the wheel. The coefficient of friction may be between 0.6 and 0.8; the load is the static weight plus or minus the variation in load of the spring.

The variation in load of the spring may be due to CF, positive or negative acceleration, aerodynamic effects, brake or power torque reaction, and, of course, unevenness of the road surface.

It is apparent that we should, on the whole, try to minimize these variations of loading, by accurate weight distribution, use of body shapes with zero lift coefficient, suitable spring linkages, and the use of soft springs, properly damped to minimize the effect of road unevenness. The hard suspension associated with sports cars will not be tolerated in the future.

We will not discuss the various spring linkages: each one is chosen by some manufacturer and it would not be fair criticism. However, it can be pointed out that a linkage which tilts the wheels, or alters the track, or interferes with the steering geometry, can only be satisfactory if the springs are fairly rigid, thus defeating the requirement of 'soft-springing'. These features have also been responsible for the excessive tyre wear which is so general with IFS.

It can also be pointed out that the car which has the best cornering capacity to date, the small Alfa Romeo 1500 cc GP, has fore and aft links on its front wheels. That is about the only system which permits the use of soft springs without introducing tyre scrub and gyroscopic effects, or steering interference. This system has also been used with a torsion bar by Auto-Union, but the coil system has many advantages.

The rear wheels should be just as well located as the front, but as the rear springs need not be quite as soft as the front springs (this can easily be demonstrated but the equations required would be out of place in this article), independent springing does not give quite the same improvement on the rear as on the front wheels. A light rear axle, located by a torque tube and a side strut with coil springs to decrease unsprung weight, may be considered a very useful compromise between the best theoretical layout and practical simplicity.

Whenever discussing springing, dampers or shock absorbers should not be forgotten. Shock absorbers have nearly as much to do with the good or bad suspension of a car as the springs themselves. In a fast car they should be well up to their job of preventing fade in a long run. The levered piston variety of the hydraulic type with pressure recuperation is about the best for the vehicles under consideration, but in some cases additional friction types may be useful. It is worthwhile remembering that a good and well proportioned hydraulic shock absorber with pressure recuperation is very nearly self adjusting, while a frictional damper is nothing of the sort. The former can be fitted, adjusted and left, but the second requires some means of adjustment by the driver, such as 'Telecontrol'.

Now that we have a car holding the road, comfortable to its driver and going where its driver desires, we can start to think about how to push it along and then how to stop it.

The total power required at the wheels is divided into:

(a) Air resistance

$$hp = \frac{A \times V^3}{374} \times k$$

Where k is a coefficient equalling 0.0018 for an open car of the old sports car type; 0.0008 for a very well streamlined saloon, and 0.0004 for a good records attempt car; A is the frontal area of the vehicle in square feet, and V is the speed in mph.

(b) The power to overcome rolling resistance given by

$$hp \text{ (rolling resistance)} = \frac{V \times W}{p^a \times 1520} \times \frac{245.6V^b}{397 \times p^{1.44}}$$

Where V is the speed of the car in mph; W is the weight of car as tested in lb; and p is the tyre pressure in psi; a is a figure relating to a particular tyre and is determined by tyre size, section construction and rubber compound; b is determined by the type and quality of road surface.*

Up to a few years ago, the rolling resistance was assumed as independent of speed, say 40 lb per ton on good roads, and therefore the power required to overcome rolling resistance was assumed to be merely proportional to speed. For low speed and with high pressure tyres it is nearly so, but at higher speeds with fairly soft tyres the equation given should be used.

This equation was determined after tedious work for use with racing tyres as used before the war: tyres with nylon cords, artificial rubber or of materially different design may show marked variations.

(c) The reserve of power, which will give life to a car.

The force required to produce an acceleration a is equal to $\dfrac{a\,W}{g}$

and the corresponding power in hp at a speed V is equal to $\dfrac{a\,W\,V}{370\,g}$

Author's note: This formula has long fallen into disuse, as progress in the field of tyre design and development has been rapid and considerable. Today more exact data on tyre performance is available from major tyre manufacturers, as a result of their attempts to improve fuel consumption.

where a is the acceleration feet/sec/sec; W is the weight of the car as tested; V is the speed at which the acceleration is considered; and g is the gravitational constant.

In order to have an acceleration of 5 feet/sec/sec at 10 mph with a car weighing 2,500 lb when tested, 10.5 bhp is required at the wheels as a reserve of power; in order to have the same acceleration at 80 mph, the reserve of power at that speed must be 84 bhp. Furthermore, whilst the air resistance in bhp in both cases, with a car having k = 0.0018 and a frontal area of 14 ft, will be .07 and 36 respectively, the power required by the rolling resistance will be 2 bhp and 25 bhp respectively, using tyres of pre-war pattern, pumped at 20 psi. Thus we shall have:

bhp *at wheel*	*at 10 mph*	*at 80 mph*
to overcome air resistance:	0.07	36
to overcome rolling resistance:	2	25
reserve of power required to give an acceleration of 5 ft/sec/sec:	10.50	84
total power required at the wheels:	12.57	145

The engine has to develop 10 or 20 per cent more power to take account of transmission losses.

It is clear that the engine must develop a lot of power at rpm corresponding to high road speeds. This explains why cars developed as sports cars by firms without previous experience are usually so disappointing. In order to give it a good bottom end performance in top gear, the car is undergeared and the engine strangled so that it cannot breathe at higher rpm, while the moving parts are so heavy that pumping and frictional horse power increase out of all proportion. Thus, whilst the car may be fairly lively up to about 50 mph, it becomes increasingly sluggish at higher speeds and more or less dies on one at 60 mph, even if it is eventually capable of 75 mph. Wear and tear at high speed are high and fuel consumption ridiculous – quite a high price to pay for that 10 mph top gear performance!

A good portion of our power is used up by air resistance. With a well streamlined saloon, we may have to face an increase of frontal area to say 15 ft, but if we can reduce our k to 0.0008, the air power at 80 mph will be decreased to 17 bhp and the total power needed to arrive at 80 mph will be reduced from 61 to 42 bhp. Given the same weight and the same acceleration of 5 ft/sec/sec, the total power will be reduced from 145 to 126 bhp.

Had we tried to save the same amount of power by weight reduction, we would have had to have saved 300 lb, thus having a complete vehicle weighing 2,200 lb. It is impossible to have high speed performance without proper streamlining – but I do mean streamlining, not the addition of chromium motifs and chromium strips along the waist line.

The design of the engine, whether supercharged or not, cannot be discussed here in detail, but I would say:

(a) The crankshaft should be as short, rigid and light as possible.

(b) The crankcase should be a really rigid structure.

(c) Valves should be as large as possible, ports well shaped and cooled, and valve gear light and rigid.

Unless (a) and (b) are satisfied, the engine will not be capable of running for long periods at high speed and high loads: its main and connecting rod bearings will see to that! Unless (c) is satisfied – and the best solution is to use a hemispherical head, with two in-line valves – the engine will not breathe easily at high rpm and the power will thus be limited.

An engine of this type must work at high bmep and high maximum pressure. To avoid blown gaskets, deformation and chewed valves, the cylinder head and top deck of the block must be rigid and the studs well distributed and 'waisted'. The use of a fixed head is to be deprecated, since it puts a limit on valve size when using a hemispherical head.

Little doubt can be entertained on the comparative efficiencies of various shapes of head. Figures obtained from racing engines and aero engines prove the hemisphere to be the best shape beyond all doubt, even if poor designs resulting from the conversion of side-valve units roughen up some engines which cannot stand the additional power. The main design of a hemispherical head is so simple, and the gas and water passages are so clean, that production staff can find little to grumble about. Messrs Riley (Coventry) Ltd have shown for many a year how effective it can be even in a relatively inexpensive design.

The number of cylinders is, of course, related to the power of the engine: the lightest engine for a given power is not the one with the largest number of very small cylinders, even if the maximum power for a given capacity may be developed by the engine with the most cylinders. We must bear in mind that the capacity of a cylinder increases as the third power of the linear dimensions, whilst the area of the said cylinder increases only as the second power.

The power developed per cycle is, within limits, proportional to the capacity, heat losses to cooling water, and friction losses due to oil shear between piston and cylinder. We can therefore see that whilst the power developed increases as the third power of a linear dimension (say the cylinder bore), a very substantial part of the losses increase only as the second power. The large cylinder will therefore be more efficient.

With the fuels we can reasonably expect after the war, about the best compromise is 25–40 bhp per cylinder. Aeroplane engine cylinders develop up to and over 160 bhp each but they have to work over a narrow range of speed and so vibrations are also in a fairly narrow range.

A lot can be said about stroke/bore ratio: the square engine is lighter but with modern fuels and high compression ratios loses more due to difficulties with combustion space shape than is otherwise gained: if the engine is supercharged matters are different, but the value of the stroke/bore ratio should be chosen according to the compression ratio of the engine. I would choose a four-cylinder engine of 2–2.5 litres having a stroke/bore ratio of 1–1.3.

Regarding transmission, I think that good synchromesh with remote control in the right position will satisfy the requirements of the sports car for a long time yet, although I have driven some excellent examples of the Cotal electrical controlled gear box.

Brakes should be powerful, progressive and, more than anything else, *consistent.* To have consistency the drum should be really rigid, the shoes well supported, and a good means of cooling must be provided. Fins outside the drum are of material help to increase rigidy but not much good as dissipators: air scoops are much better.

The front brake will do over 70 per cent of the work and must therefore be bigger and better cooled than the rear. A lot can be said for all brake control systems: personally I think the hydraulic is the best, providing the plumbing is carefully installed and kept away from the exhaust pipes.

Air brakes or spoilers may be quite useful on streamlined cars and materially ease the life of the main brake.

Of the cars that have been made and marketed as sports cars, very few can really claim to be such. The Riley 9 Brooklands model was perhaps the best amongst the small ones: the late Mr Percy Riley, who developed the original modifications, turned out a vehicle that in its day was far and away better than anything similar. The little Riley had a number of imitators, here and abroad, but none ever achieved a comparable performance. I had the pleasure of handling one of these in an International Alpine Trial and its superiority over foreign sports cars of similar size was very marked.

This country unfortunately was more famous for its 'fast lorries' than its sports cars, but one other vehicle which can truly claim to be a sports car was the 4½ Invicta. That car could meet Continental competitors on their own ground or even beat them. In the Coupe des Alpes and the Monte Carlo Rally, etc., it proved better than their best.

Both these cars were hard sprung, but that was the best we knew in those days. The remarkable power to weight ratio also caused some difficulty. Dr A C Sampietro, who was associated with Mr Reid Railton and whom I consider to be one of the few engineers in this country capable of designing a high performance car, always said that in the case of both the Riley and the Invicta, trouble was caused when second-rate drivers took first-class risks.

Another car I have admired in its day was the Talbot 95. The steadiness, performance and reliability of these cars was wonderful to watch and Mr Georges Roesch proved to be one of the best of the few designers in this country who understood what a sports car should be.

Amongst the Continental models I cannot but recall the perfection of the SSK Mercedes, the agility of the 1750 Six-cylinder Alfa, and the 2300 eight-cylinder Bugatti, but my admiration is now reserved for the 2900 eight-cylinder Alfa Romeo. Speed, acceleration, road holding, comfort of ride, perfection of control are all there: what a pity there is not a British design to touch, nay to better it!

Unfortunately most British designs to date have been adaptions of family-type car chassis sold under another name, and the results have been very disappointing to the real enthusiast. The large manufacturer is naturally not interested in a market for say 500 to 1,000 cars per year; he has not the technique to produce the designs and a sideline in a big organization is always a failure. We have a few designers with sufficient *road experience* – and I stress this as it is completely lacking in most chief designers of large organizations – to design a car of the type described. But let us hope that a way may be found to produce such a car economically and regain British prestige in a market we have lost to the Continental manufacturers.

This article by DMH, written 35 years ago, outlined principles that were relevant when the Austin Healey was created and that are still valid today, although the gap between sports car and normal passenger car handling has since narrowed considerably as the major manufacturers have improved their products.

The first Healey cars were known officially as the Healey 2.4 litre Roadster and the Healey 2.4 litre Saloon. Both models were powered by the 2.4 litre Riley engine and built on the same chassis, designed by Sammy Sampietro. The bodies were designed by Ben Bowden and featured a low vertical front face that formed, unknown to us, an air dam – a feature recently rediscovered by motor manufacturers. The cars were very fast for their day, comfortably exceeding 100 mph on an engine output of 100 bhp.

Inside the small workshop at Benfords in Warwick. Ben Bowden, the author, and Peter McClure working on the first car.

2.4-litre clutch pedal RR56 light alloy forging. This was identical to the brake pedal forging, with an offset to one side added as a second operation.

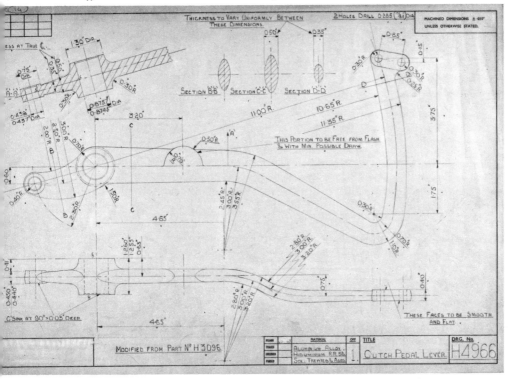

Ben Bowden, the stylist and body engineer, with the first Healey Saloon on Alpine development.

It was a hard struggle to design and construct a new car at the end of the war. Steel was in very short supply and available only on permit, for exports which would earn hard currency. The first Healeys used a large amount of aluminium alloy, much of which was in the form of Hiduminium forgings. Hiduminium is a registered trade name of High Duty Alloys, a Hawker Siddeley company, and they provided us with high-strength aircraft alloy forgings for the front suspension parts, and the brake and clutch levers. The brake pedal was a true work of art, being exceptionally light and strong. These components never failed throughout their production life.

Sammy Sampietro's chassis design was first-rate, being cheap to produce and involving little expenditure on tooling. The main members were folded sections produced on a brake press. The torsional rigidity of the frame was high for its day – much higher than that used on any other contemporary sports or open car. We were to use the figures we obtained by torsionally testing this frame at Warwick as a guide for future designs.

The Westland Motor Company and Aero Parts Engineering, both run by CH Shelton of Hereford, were responsible for manufacturing the chassis frames and much of the machining work, and also built the Roadster bodies. For both companies, the project marked the change-over from essential war work. The quality of Aero Parts' machining was very high, a tradition they maintain to this day. The first experimental Roadster body was an exception, as it was built so soon after the end of the war that no body builders were then available. DMH arranged for Riley to build it in their experimental body shop at Coventry and it was later mounted by Westland onto chassis number two. The first and all subsequent Saloon bodies were built by Samuel Elliott and Sons of Reading.

The engines were built either by Eddie Maher's team at Riley (Morris Motors) or by Roger Menadue. The Riley engine was generally a very reliable unit, apart from its tendency to oil surge in the sump under hard cornering. This would lead to a lack of oil supply to the big end bearings and their subsequent failure. Roger and Eddie devised a special oil pan baffling which overcame this problem.

Despite the use of large hydraulic dampers, the cars always suffered from lack of damping during extended competition use. Their roadholding and handling were exceptionally good for the period, probably being bettered only by the Ferraris and Maseratis. Even so, the forward mounted engine and trailing link front suspension resulted in a large amount of understeer, which made traversing an Alpine pass really hard work for the driver.

The Cape of Good Hope, the pub on the canal bank in Warwick, with the first Healey.

Egypt in 1947. Siphoning petrol from a tank in order to get fuel to run a car.

My first car: an Austin Seven two-seater.

My contribution to the new car was to spend part of my leave from the
army welding up the rear of the chassis, putting the knowledge I had
recently acquired at an army welding course to good use. My best
remembered experience of that first chassis was the large front wheel
movement and soft suspension. It had a total of 8 inches of wheel travel
from full bump to full rebound. My other most vivid memory is of the poor
quality of the tyres then available. Few high speed runs could be completed
without a tyre bursting – although DMH would still continue to control the
vehicle with his customary apparent ease. Wartime difficulties necessitated
the use of recycled rubber and dubious synthetic rubbers in the construction
of tyres. All the accompanying design and supply problems were overcome
by Dunlop, however, who proceeded to produce a tyre capable of
withstanding speeds in excess of 100 mph with complete reliability. Con-
structional integrity was the first requirement, followed by wet grip and long
life.

The First Healeys

On my demobilization in 1947 (the Government delayed demobilization for those serving in the Middle East because of the difficulties in providing employment), I joined Armstrong Siddeley Motors in Coventry, as DMH considered that I needed more experience before I joined the family business. At Armstrong Siddeley I was fortunate to come into contact with some of the great men of the industry, such as W O Bentley, who was then acting as a consultant to the company on the design of a new car. Many excellent engineers, including Mervyn Cutler, John Densham, Doug de Launte and Ken Stansbury, were working on the new project, which featured a 3-litre double overhead camshaft six-cylinder engine, designed by Bentley and Bastow. There was great disappointment when Siddeley decided not to go ahead with the engine, for it had already achieved 125 bhp at 5,200 rpm on its early test bed runs. It was during this period that MIRA, the Motor Industry Research Association, opened its test ground at Lindley, outside Coventry: over the next 30 years, we were to test and develop many motor cars here, under the watchful eyes of Ossie Dolby, the test track manager.

My second car: a 3-litre Bentley bought for £28 in 1945.

Above: *The Hot Rod, inspired by an American trip and built with Healey bits from the scrap heap, with a Ford V8 engine from a Bren Carrier. It made fastest time of the day in its only event.*

Above right: *The Red Bug in Italy.*

Competition played a crucial role in the development of the Healey cars, right from the very start. A number of production Roadsters and Saloons were specially prepared for individual races and rallies, the responsibility for this work being one of the many functions of Roger Menadue. Two cars were prepared for 1948: a Roadster, and a Saloon stripped of its sliding roof to save weight. The Saloon was driven by Count Johnny Lurani and Dorino Serafini in the Targa Florio, where it finished thirteenth overall and first in class. With the same car and with Carlo Sandri as co-driver, Lurani also achieved an identical position in the 1948 Mille Miglia road race, winning the touring car class. Johnny Lurani was a great international sportsman, who helped us on many occasions. He would have finished very much higher up in the results if the track bar or Panhard rod which provided lateral locations for the rear axle had not torn away from the chassis frame. This made the car oversteer violently. I certainly did not enjoy driving it back to England after the race.

DMH and I drove the Roadster in this same Mille Miglia. We soon discovered that the racing tyres provided by Dunlop, with their very stiff sidewalls and hard rubber compound treads, gave little grip on the wet Italian roads. The sensation was one of driving on ice. Fortunately, Johnny was able to arrange the supply of some Pirelli tyres for the race. These were very different, with supple sidewalls and a comparatively soft tread rubber, giving good wet grip. Tyre development over the years has been tremendous and driving on these old tyres would scare the best of today's drivers. Before half-distance our dynamo failed, one of the very rare occasions on which we had trouble with Lucas equipment. This was to worry us in the

The first Healey car, taken to the USA by DMH and the author in 1948.

A Healey Roadster outside Los Angeles, during our US tour in 1948.

later stages of the race when we could not use the lights. In the last 200 miles, if we switched them on, the engine cut out. We had one incident when a large dog ran across the road and we struck it, bursting a tyre and damaging the right-hand wing. Bent Birmabright is nasty stuff to straighten out and we lost valuable time hammering the wing away from the wheel. The brakes also proved to be unsuitable for racing, due in part to the bodywork cutting off the flow of cooling air. Despite these problems, we finished ninth overall and fourth in the unlimited sports car class. The Mille Miglia was a thoroughly enjoyable race, which gave one a chance to compare the performance of the car against the best sports cars of the day.

DMH was keen to produce a more sporting machine and this resulted in X1, the 96-inch wheel-base two-seater. Known as the Red Bug, this was essentially a standard chassis with the wheel base shortened by 6 inches. The engine remained well forward in its four-seater position, with the torque tube reduced in length by 6 inches. The rear suspension was modified with Lockheed air struts replacing the coil springs and hydraulic shock absorbers. This early attempt at air suspension, the brainchild of Peter Thornhill, had certain shortcomings. There was excessive seal friction and the suspension height varied with temperature. These units were only used experimentally on a few cars, including Standard Vanguards and BRM Racing cars. The Red Bug was also the first Healey car to be fitted with Dunlop centre lock wire wheels. The bodywork was mainly constructed by Gerry Turner's Cape Engineering works in Warwick, entirely in metal, using light alloy panels on a tubular steel framework. The forward position of the power unit made styling a problem and the aggressive-looking car could not be described as attractive.

DMH took this car to north Italy, meeting Sammy at one of his family's hotels for tests on Alpine passes. During this DMH picked up a nasty virus infection which the brilliant young Doctor Volpati succeeded in curing, though it was a close thing. Sammy, then a pretty wild driver, drove the bug back to Warwick at high speed. His description of the drive would reduce everyone to hysterics.

The car was sold to the racing driver Curly Dryden, who kept the George Inn at Dorchester on the Thames near Abingdon. Eddie Maher later built up a 2-litre version of the 2.4, fitted with an 8 port head and high compression, to run on methanol based fuel, and Curly raced this car with some success.

After this experience of the Red Bug and its shortcomings, DMH started thinking about a new two-seater sports car. He laid down a new outline design incorporating the normal 102-inch wheelbase chassis, with the engine and occupants located further back to provide better weight distribution. The detailed design of the car was the work of Len Hodges, a

The First Healeys

Above right: *Tommy Wisdom in a Silverstone at Silverstone. (Guy Griffiths)*
Above left: *DMH tried most things, including skiing at St Moritz.*

This Silverstone driven by Tommy Wisdom was one of three cars to take the team prize in the Silverstone production car race.

brilliant but somewhat absent-minded engineer. He was also responsible for the design and engineering of the entire body. The prototype was X2, the first of the Healey Silverstones which have since become collectors' pieces. The body of this car and subsequent production models was built by Abbey Panels in Coventry, who also did a great deal of body work for Jaguar. DMH and Ian Appleyard of Jaguar fame drove this car in the 1949 Alpine Rally to second overall position and first in class.

The next month three Silverstones were entered in the Silverstone production car race. Engines of that era had a nasty habit of losing core plugs. Sometimes known as freeze plugs, these were used to fill holes in the water jacket of the cylinder block and head. These holes were necessary to facilitate the positioning of the sand cores used when the blocks were cast. One of the Silverstones, driven by Tony Rolt, blew out a core plug when I was less than a mile from the works. It was in an awkward position, at the rear of the cylinder block, and it was fortunate that it came out before the race. Roger cut a hole in the bulkhead and managed to hammer in a new one with the latest jointing compound. The entry of the three Silverstones took the team prize for the *Daily Express* production car race Tony Rolt coming fourth overall behind two Jaguars and a Frazer-Nash.

Silverstones proved popular with the racing fraternity. Robin Richards, Edgar Wadsworth, Onslow Bartlett, Peter Riley, Peter Simpson and

Another view of the Cadillac V8 engine with Ford gearbox in a Silverstone chassis. In order to reduce bonnet height, two SU carburettors were later fitted.

Charles Mortimer all raced and rallied them, and Charles Mortimer has written a very good book about his exploits. Some were exported to the USA. Briggs Cunningham had two, one of which he modified to take a Cadillac V8 – the first American engine to be fitted to a Healey. Briggs took second overall with this car at Palm Beach, Florida in 1950 while Phil Walter finished fifth in the other standard Silverstone. The Briggs Cunningham car is still in America and has been restored by its present owner, Don Barrow.

Briggs Cunningham's success prompted us to ask him to arrange for us to obtain a Cadillac V8. Bill Frick of Frick Tappet Motors supplied us with all the details of the bits that were needed to fit it into a Silverstone. This car, X4, was built up by Roger. The rear axle was a Ford torque tube unit fitted with a Colombia quick change centre to give suitable gear ratios. The gearbox was a three-speed Ford unit: with the high torque output of the Cadillac, strength was more important than a multiplicity of gears. The car had very good acceleration but the maximum speed was not high due to its poor aerodynamic shape. SU provided two 45° carburettors which were fitted in a similar manner to that used by Rover on their V8.

The Cadillac engine and Ford three-speed gearbox, plus the Colombia quick change axle centre, arrived in boxes from the USA. A Silverstone chassis frame was blocked up to its normal ride height and the Ford axle

The Cadillac V8 engine in a Silverstone chassis. The front suspension was very expensive, with its cast elektron spacers, forged aluminium suspension arms, and needle and ball bearings.

Tommy Wisdom approaching the finish of the 1949 Mille Miglia. The front air dam effect is evident. Although this was good for speed, the brakes did not like the lack of cooling air.

positioned in the car. This axle was obtained from our local Ford dealer, C H Soans & Sons. Ford were then practising their 'world car concept', and common or very similar axles and V8 power units were available in all parts of the globe. Roger cut and shut the torque tube to allow the power unit to sit in the desired fore and aft position. A local machine shop cut the propeller shaft down and remachined the splines on one end. Silverstone brakes were adapted to the rear axle with hubs to take the Healey disc wheels. The Cadillac engine was assembled to the Ford gearbox with the use of a Frick adapter plate. Some of the chassis frame members were cut away to provide clearance and Roger and I soon schemed out how to fix the engine with some simple folded steel brackets.

The whole project was tackled with very little design or drawing office involvement and as a result it was completed very quickly. Exhaust headers were fabricated to marry up with a Silverstone silencer on either side of the chassis frame. One advantage of the Silverstone body structure was that it was a one-piece unit with its own framing, and could thus be lifted straight onto the chassis frame and secured with a few nuts and bolts. The most difficult operation was to get one's head and shoulders through the spare wheel aperture in order to fit the rear mounting bolts. Briggs Cunningham went one stage further by cutting and adapting the front end so that this could be removed for engine work, a decided improvement for racing.

Roger and I tried the car on trade plates on the local roads. There was very little that needed changing. With double the torque and 50 per cent more power, the Cadillac engine was sensational. The Ford drive line was much smoother than the Healey assembly. The car was very rapid off the mark, with an excess of power making it possible to spin the rear wheels in all gears. The handling was better than that of the normal Silverstone although the rear end would break away too easily under power.

We were considering running the car in the Mille Miglia when Count Aymo Maggi and Commendatore Renzo Castagneto of the Brescia Automobile Club arrived in England with Aldo Bassi. Bassi was an experienced Mille Miglia driver from Brescia, who was looking for a drive in a car with the potential to win the race. A quick phone call and we had Gaydon available for a test. With some trepidation I sat in the passenger's seat and explained the controls and rev limits. Bassi took off down the perimeter track and put the car to its limits, with the rear end hanging out on all the bends. After six laps he declared he had done enough. Translated into English, his remarks amounted to: 'It's good. It will be very quick in the mountains but on the long straights the Ferrari will go past Zut! Zut! Zut!, and you must fit Pirelli's to get more grip.' He was obsessed, like all Italian drivers of the day, with winning the Mille Miglia. Drivers who won the race could justifiably claim to be the greatest of road race drivers. The

A Silverstone chassis with a Wade supercharger mounted in front. The long inlet tract resulted in a delay in throttle response. This modification did not increase the Silverstone's performance as much as had been anticipated.

list of past winners speaks for itself – Minoia, Campari, Nuvolari, Carraciola, Borzacchini, Varzi, Pintacuda, Brivio, Biondetti, Von Hanstein, Marzotto, Villoresi, Bracco, Ascari, Moss, Castelloti and Taruffi. Bassi was subsequently offered a drive in a Ferrari which he naturally accepted, finishing sixth overall. DMH and I realized that the Cadillac was too quick for us and we chose instead the more staid and comfortable Saloon and Roadster models.

I received an invitation to run the Cadillac at the Bank Holiday Hill Climb at Trengwainton in Cornwall. Inevitably the road was wet and slippery and I was not able to do full justice to its power, but it was a fun outing.

This whole project was finally dropped because DMH was unable to arrange a supply of Cadillac engines. The body of X4 was removed and the running chassis sold to Portugal. A Portuguese driver had managed to

45

obtain an import licence for a chassis and at that time bodies were easy to build.

DMH was determined to break into the American market as he saw little future in Europe for sports cars. He set sail for the USA on the *Queen Elizabeth* with the intention of arranging a supply of Cadillac engines. On board he met George Mason of Nash Motors, on his way back from Europe. DMH and George Mason discussed the automobile industry at length and DMH naturally told George the reason for his visit. He replied that the boss of the Cadillac division was an old friend and that he would give him an introduction. However, he warned DMH that Cadillac could not meet the demand for engines for their own cars and suggested that he should come back to Nash and see what they had to offer.

DMH was well received in Detroit but, as George had indicated, they did not have enough engines to satisfy their own needs and were unable to help. So the next port of call was Nash Motors in Kenosha, Wisconsin, where he had long meetings with the Nash Motors chiefs. Nash wanted to do more than supply engines; they wanted DMH to build sports cars for them, using Nash units in Silverstone chassis. They wanted a prestige car, a limited production sports car to raise interest in their own product and draw customers into the dealers' showrooms. They were astute enough to realize that for a comparatively small investment they would add glamour to the Nash name and rejuvenate sales.

DMH discussed engineering details with Meade F Moore and selected the units needed for a prototype. He returned to Warwick armed with all the necessary detail drawings, an agreement to build the cars, and the bare bones of a competition programme. This was the start of a period of cooperation with Nash Motors which, though not particularly long, was to prove immensely fruitful, representing one of the most important turning points in the history of the Healey marque.

The Nash Healey
Specials

The Nash Healey played a very important role in the Healey story. The marque's many competition successes and consequent exposure enabled us to become properly established, for the first time, in the all important American market, and the association with Nash also generated the cash that was to enable us to produce the Healey Hundred.

Our first priority was to scheme the engine, gearbox and Nash rear axle into a modified Silverstone chassis. It was immediately apparent that we would need a shorter torque tube and drive shaft and we sent details of these to Kenosha: on the next boat, we receive all the Nash components we required. John Thompson were making the Silverstone chassis and they quickly produced a modified chassis frame for the car. Roger devised a floor-mounted gear shift mechanism for the gearbox. The Silverstone body was modified to give it greater width and an air intake was fitted in the bonnet lid to provide clearance over the rocker cover on the tall Nash engine. The engine was a conventional six-cylinder, long stroke, overhead valve design with a seven-main-bearing crankshaft and cast iron cylinder head. The gearbox was a three-speed unit with a Borg Warner overdrive at the rear. The standard unit had a single downdraft carburettor. Our good friends at Armstrong Siddeley Motors agreed to put the first unit on the test bed and give it a full power test. Siddeley's development engineer, Ken Stansbury, carried out a full investigation and reported the output as 103 bhp at 3,700 rpm with a maximum torque of 184 lb/ft at 1,200 rpm – a typical low-speed slogger which would need a bit of improvement for sports car use.

SU's carburation expert, Edward Boyle, came and advised us on where we could best fit two 1¾ SU carburettors to the head. A new manifold cover was cast that would carry the upper mounting bolts of the carburettors. Roger then cut through the side of the head into the inlet gallery and screwed on two steel plates to take the lower mounting bolts. This plate was sealed to the iron head casting with cast iron cement.

The whole operation – modifying parts and constructing the prototype, X5 – was carried out at break-neck speed with the aim of running in the Mille Miglia. The dates in the diaries are as follows:

1950 – February 16: body delivered to Warwick.
                       26: Nash parts arrived.
          April   5: Car road tested.
                       7 Good Friday: set off for Cornwall – work all Saturday rectifying cooling system.
                       16 Leave for Mille Miglia.
                       23 Mille Miglia Road Race.
                       27 Back in Warwick.

When looking back over the past, one always wonders how cars could be designed, built and run in such a short time. The probable reasons are that cars were simpler and there were fewer regulations to be met. In addition, we were not hampered by non-productive people such as product planners, build engineers, programmers and trade union officials: DMH had suffered enough at the hands of obstinate draughtsmen and they had no place in our organization. The working week averaged 55 hours, with the occasional free weekend and two weeks annual holiday with a bit of luck.

The planned test run to Cornwall was terminated by engine overheating, so we went back and called Roger in from his Easter break, to modify the cooling system. During the test run it had appeared that the water flow through the radiator ran through only one portion of the core and we therefore split the outlet from the cylinder head into two pipes, feeding into opposite ends of the radiator header tank. This we called the ram's horn water outlet – and it certainly cured the problem. We completed the 500-mile test in typical wet Easter weather. Compared to a Silverstone, the Nash Healey, with its weighty six at the front, had excellent directional stability but the front end would tend to plough straight on at corners. The rear axle arrangement was superior to the Silverstone, displaying less tendency to rear wheel hop and hanging on much longer under high cornering forces. It was an easier car to drive fast although as it was more ponderous than the Silverstone, it would be slower on tight circuits.

On the following Sunday we left for the night ferry to Europe, DMH and I in the Nash Healey, with Roger, Dunlop Mac and a pile of spares in a Standard Vanguard estate, loaned to us by Ted Grinham of Standard

Motors. In France we decided that the exhaust system could be improved and with the aid of a local blacksmith, we made a new three-branch exhaust manifold. Our next stop was at the Sampietro Grand Hotel at Tremezzo, where we met members of the British Press, coming to the race. It was here that I met my wife Margot for the first time.

The Italian petrol was of much higher octane rating than that available in England and we decided to raise the compression ratio of the engine by getting the cylinder head face machined. Margot, with her fluent Italian, was pressed into service for the first of many such times, to arrange for this work to be done at the FIAT garage in Como. FIAT garages were something special, having excellent machine shops and skilled machinists available. The massive cast iron Nash head was machined on the largest planer they had. We were afraid we would be charged heavily for this work, but Margot was expert at haggling with Italians and the invoice was an agreeable surprise. We went on to Brescia for the scrutineering, carried out by a number of very friendly and helpful Italian experts from Italian motor companies.

We looked on the Mille Miglia as one of the best possible tests of a motor car, with the added advantage that it allowed one to hide any shortcomings in a car's performance from the outside world. X5 did have shortcomings. It was slow, with a maximum speed of not much over 100 mph. Any prolonged high speed would cause the oil temperature to rise to a dangerously high figure. DMH drove hard but with one eye on the oil temperature gauge, which meant that we had to lose time on the long, very fast straights. We obviously would not finish very high up and we would have to think up a good story to hide the truth of the car's poor performance. The 1,000 mile route of the Mille Miglia attracts many spectators and we happened to see some monks and novices in the mountains around Florence. We then devised a story about being forced off the road and having a group of wandering monks lift the car back onto it. The story went down well and became a piece of Healey history! Ted Eves, who knows more about motor racing in Europe than most journalists, was sceptical as usual, pointing out that the nearest monastery was some 100 miles away. This was probably bluff on his part, as I doubt that he knew the location of all Italian monasteries.

DMH flew back immediately after the race, impatient as ever to get on with the projects in hand, while I spent a few days at Tremezzo, chatting up the interpreter, before driving the car back to England.

We had entered X5 in the 1950 Le Mans race in June and we now needed to find some speed quickly. Sammy Sampietro, now a part-time consultant to the company, contributed the design of a camshaft designed to raise the engine output and its speed range. Cecil Winby, BRICO's piston expert,

The Nash Healey 1950 Le Mans car, showing the flared wings, head rest and screen. It finished fourth overall.

examined the pistons and came up with a new ring set to reduce friction loss and decrease blow-by, the cause of the high oil temperature. Roger rebuilt the engine with the new camshaft and piston rings and our good friends at Armstrong Siddely put the engine on their test beds for a couple of days. Ken Stansbury obtained 126 bhp at 4,600 rpm – a much more promising output, though still well down on what Wally Hassan was getting at Jaguar.

The Le Mans regulations decreed that the wings should be integral with the body and so our local panel beater, Bill Buckingham, was called in to join them up and to produce the extensions that made the bodywork all enveloping. Once all the little details required by the regulations had been fitted, such as the leather bonnet strap, DMH and I took the car out early one wet Sunday morning to the straight piece of the A5 near Daventry. At this time there were few people about and few police patrols, and it was safe to try the car for maximum speed. It was much faster, indicating 124 mph without too much difficulty.

Tom Kenny, our French agent, made all the arrangements, including booking us in at a Chateau outside Le Mans, where Nigel Mann and Mort Goodall were based. Tony Rolt was to be our number one driver and his partner would be Duncan Hamilton. We had toyed with the idea of using a young man who was driving very well that year – Stirling Moss, but were a little apprehensive of his lack of experience in long distance races. The team consisted of the drivers, with their wives doing the victualling and time keeping, Tom Kenny running the pits, Francois Cueillièr doing the refuelling, and Roger and I as the mechanics, assisted by Sacco (John

Saxton) and Peter Thornhill. Harry Costley of Nash came to watch their investment.

The car ran well in the early stages, getting up to third place, but while slowing for Mulsanne its rear was struck by a brakeless Delage, which damaged it badly. The axle was pushed forward and the exhaust system broken. Roger swiped some local telephone wire and secured the exhaust. Now, after being in with a chance of winning, we had to concentrate on finishing.

At the last pit stop, Dunlop's racing manager came to make a check on the tyres. He was either bloody minded or over-cautious – slowly examining each tyre and making us change them all. The car did the last four hours without incident, finishing fourth overall. Everyone was pretty happy, apart from Harry Costley who thought we ought to have won. Nash used the result in a large advertising campaign which cost considerably more than the whole Nash Healey project.

A few hours after leaving Le Mans, on the return to England, the engine stopped and would not restart. The crankshaft had broken in the rear bearing, probably as a result of the rear end shunt which had bent the rear of the engine. This engine was subsequently rebuilt with a new crank and rear main bearing cap. It is not normally possible to fit a new bearing cap to an engine without line boring, but Roger succeeded with a little filing and the engine was pressed back into service.

We now had a clearer picture of what Le Mans was all about and designed a new car for 1951. DMH and Gerry Coker designed a streamlined fixed top coupé, making full use of Armstrong Whitworth's help over the aerodynamics. Lionel Rawson at Slough constructed the body on the X5 Nash Healey chassis frame. This featured a quickly detachable escape hatch in the roof, flush push-button door locks, Clayton Wright rubber glazing and a vast 40 gallon fuel tank. This car was renumbered X6, with the Nash number NH2023. The small Lockheed $11 \times 1\frac{3}{4}$ front and $10 \times 1\frac{3}{4}$ rear brakes were replaced with some special $11 \times 2\frac{1}{4}$ Girling twin trailing shoe brakes, with an automatic adjustant for wear.

The type of construction then used, with a chassis frame to which a body was bolted, meant that we were able to change bodies and chassis very easily. We swopped these around frequently, often using the same registration plates. It was very much a case of saying to Roger; 'Stick some plates on that, I want to try it up the road.'

At the same time, the production Nash Healeys were coming down the line at Warwick. That is, we had a line of chassis in the main hangar at the Cape and were fitting the bodies supplied by Panel Craft of Birmingham. As a result of a discussion between DMH and George Mason of Nash, the decision was taken to give the Nash Healey a more modern all-enveloping

Le Mans 1950. Tony Rolt about to leave the pits with the Nash Healey. Sacco (John Saxton) with pipe.

Tony Rolt finishing fourth at Le Mans in the 1950 Nash Healey. To our eyes and in those days, it never seemed so large and ugly. This car was the forerunner of the production Nash Healeys.

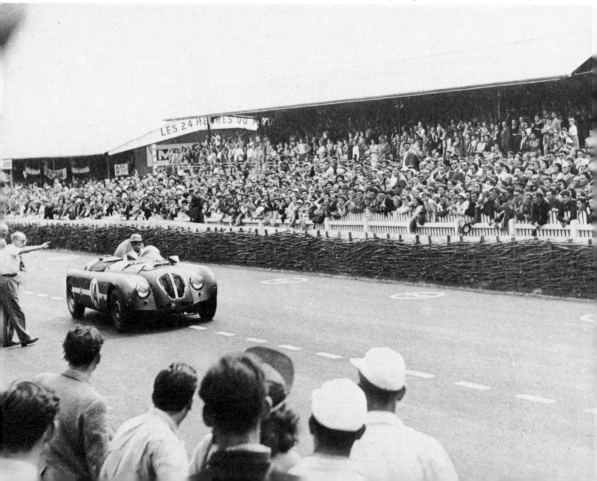

body, of a type disparagingly referred to as the 'cake of soap' concept. DMH and Len Hodges devised this body and from Len's quarter-scale drawings Gerry drew the full-size plans on a hurriedly constructed wall board. Gerry was then working full time with Sammy in his consulting business in Surrey. Nash carried out some additional work to enable us to incorporate their die-cast aluminium grille with vertical bars, as used on the 1951 Ambassador. We took one of these cars off the line and modified it for competition use.

Nash were using a grille on their 1950 Statesman that we liked better. In appearance it was not unlike the egg-box Ferrari grilles, but was of one-piece die-cast aluminium construction. It also offered less obstruction of air flow to the radiator. The production Nash Healeys had 10 inch diameter Bendix duo servo brakes that were quite useless for racing, and so these were replaced by Girling twin trailing shoe brakes using Mintex linings. The production bench type seat was heavy and devoid of sideways support and this was replaced by two production 2.4 litre Roadster seats. This car was not much heavier than the original X5 prototype and for its day was quite attractive.

DMH and I ran this car in the 1951 Mille Miglia. Although not very fast, it was comfortable with safe and predictable handling. Its good fuel consumption and very low oil consumption enabled us to complete the race with very few refuelling stops. The first dark stage was achieved at near maximum speed, thanks to the Lucas flame thrower lamps. We managed a creditable 30th overall position, with fourth in class.

This same car, using registration number KWD 947, was driven by Tony Rolt in the British Racing Drivers Club production car race at Silverstone, where it finished sixth overall. Reg Parnell borrowed the car for the British Empire Trophy Race in the Isle of Man but it was really too large and cumbersome for the narrow tricky circuit. Reg Parnell went well but had the gear lever come out in his hand. Although he rammed it back, the circlip retainer had failed: it jumped out again and so he retired.

The car was next used in the Tour de France. Our French agent, Tom Kenny, had arranged a deal for an entry in this rally which was built up to be the motoring event of the century. The car was getting somewhat tired by now, but Tom assured us that this did not matter. When I arrived in Nice for the start, the oil pressure was getting low: we dropped the sump and found that the oil pump was worn. Once we had cleaned it up and put it back, the pressure returned to normal. Part of Tom's deal was that the car should run on Michelin tyres. These were supposed to be the last word in long wearing properties, but their wet grip was nearly non-existent. The rally was a long boring affair, with very lengthy stopovers in scenic areas. The oil pressure fell off regularly but we found we could easily make up

Reg Parnell leading a Ferrari and others at the 1951 British Empire Trophy Race on the Isle of Man, with the production-bodied Nash Healey with a special radiator grille. (Guy Griffiths)

time before each timed stage, allowing us to put in a fresh fill of Castrol oil and restore the pressure. Whilst cruising down a wet road I was confronted by the rear of a van which drove out from behind a café and stopped, with an oncoming camion blocking the only way round it. Despite stopping as quickly as possible, we struck the van squarely in the rear, bending the front of the car and cracking the radiator. At the next control, we decided that the damage was such that we had no hope of winning and so we retired. The car was repaired and sold in England.

For the 1951 Le Mans, we again entered Duncan Hamilton and Tony Rolt with the coupé. Despite its heavy appearance, this car was 240 lb lighter than the Mille Miglia car, scaling 2,520 lb with 20 gallons of fuel. The 40 gallon tank when full added 300 lb to the rear wheel load but the handling was good from full to empty. The brakes demanded a pedal pressure of over 130 lb for a 90 per cent retardation and thus required strong-legged drivers. We had a choice of two gearboxes, both of American manufacture, fitted with Borg Warner overdrives. We ended up with the close ratio gearbox which at 4,500 rpm gave 140 in overdrive top, 120 in overdrive second, 100 in direct top, 87 in second and 49 in first. The highest

speed noted on the long straight was 130 mph. 1951 was the first of many times that we stayed at the Hotel du Croissant at Cerans Foulletorte, due west of the circuit. On the main road, the hotel was very noisy at night. Duncan and Tony were a natural team, with a wealth of racing experience. They drove to sixth place overall, the race being won by the new C type Jaguar at record speed. All the 1951 cars were hampered by the race officials' stupid insistence on the use of the type agrée yellow bulbs which made high speeds at night far more hazardous.

The next race would be the 1952 Mille Miglia but in between we would not be idle at Warwick. We were involved in looking for a substitute for the Riley engine which was due to go out of production. We had completed the installation of the 3 litre Alvis engine in a modified Nash Healey, known as the 'G' Type or 3 litre Healey. In addition, Pinin Farina were modernizing a Nash Healey body in Turin. I spent quite a lot of time in Turin sorting out the chassis modifications they required to suit their methods of construction. Farina's body construction methods were unique in the small volume field and their workmanship was of the highest quality. Perhaps the most significant development of all occurred late in November, when DMH obtained Len Lord's agreement to supply Austin units for a car we planned to produce – later known as the Healey Hundred.

The 1952 season opened with the Mille Miglia. DMH and I drove the Le Mans coupé while Leslie Johnson and Bill McKenzie, the motoring correspondent of the *Daily Telegraph*, drove the rebuilt 1950 Le Mans car. Both cars were fitted with the enlarged Nash engines of 4.1 litres' capacity. DMH and I crashed into a bridge in the wet, due to aquaplaning and seriously damaged the coupé, but Leslie Johnson and McKenzie went on to finish fourth in class and seventh overall. As usual, the Italians were most helpful, arranging the quick transport of the wreck back to Warwick.

DMH and I got back to Warwick to plan what to do for Le Mans. The coupé was badly damaged and we considered that it would take too long to rebuild. Instead, Roger and I schemed up a car – X8 – that could be built very quickly. With Roger's aid and ingenuity, City Street Metal of Coventry built the body onto a production Nash Healey chassis frame, with the aim of using special parts off the wreck when it returned from Italy.

The original race car, X5, was being prepared with a special engine. The limitations of the Nash engine lay in the cylinder head with its inline valves and inlet gallery cast in the cylinder head, a design that had no advantages

The Nash Healey coupé at Le Mans as the drivers line up across the narrow road for the start.

The Pinin Farina body on the Nash Healey.

and which was not unlike the head used on the early Austin Healey six-cylinder engines. Sampietro was still acting as a consultant to us and with Nash's agreement he was given the job of designing a new cylinder head. Sammy drew up a hemispherical head with valves at an included angle of 90°. There were six large inlet ports on one side and six exhaust ports on the other. The valves were operated from the camshaft in the block, the inlet valves being operated via rocker arms and the exhaust valves by way of a rocker arm and cross pushrods. Prior to the very successful adoption of overhead camshafts, as on the Jaguar, many designers tried to operate hemispherical head engines with push rods. This inevitably resulted in a very heavy head, due to the multiplicity of push rods and rockers.

The detail design and manufacture was left in the capable hands of Ken Taylor of Thompson and Taylor, whose workshops were located on the track at Brooklands. On paper, the complete engine, with its large valve area and separate straight ports, was capable of producing 190 bhp. However, time for the whole project was very limited and the only figures given to us by Ken Taylor were 155 bhp at 4,000 rpm, 160 at 4,500 and 157 at 5,000 – a goodly increase on the 135 given by the production head. The special pistons were heavy and we were worried about the extra loading on the rods and bearings.

Leslie Johnson, our number one driver, was given the choice of cars for Le Mans: X5 with the hemispherical head engine, or X8, the new light-weight car. Leslie and I tried X5 around the MIRA test track. It certainly went well, showing excellent acceleration, but the additional front end weight increased the understeering tendencies. Leslie and I decided that he would drive X8 with Tommy Wisdom, and that X5 would be given to the two French drivers, Veyron and Giraud Cabantous.

In the race a rocker shaft broke on the new engine. The rocker shafts had a valve rocker at each end beyond the support of the outer rocker pedestals. This combination of heavy loading with insufficient support was exacer-bated by the hole through the shaft for the pedestal bolt. This was bad practice and should not have been allowed, although in fact cylinder head conversions are often mechanically unsound, due to the limitations imposed by the original block and stud layout. Leslie Johnson and Tommy Wisdom kept X8 going with speed and regularity to finish third overall behind the two gull-wing Mercedes race cars.

After the race, both the cars and all the cylinder head designs were sent to Nash Motors. Nash used the race results to good effect and were interested in the head for possible production use after some real development. Their engineers came up with some modifications to improve the rocker shaft configuration but the project was eventually shelved.

Nash agreed a further racing programme for 1953 which involved the construction of two more special cars, X14 and X15, to replace the 1952 cars now in America. Gerry Coker drew up all-enveloping bodywork with large cutaways either side of the grille to help airflow to the front brakes. Laycock built two special overdrives capable of transmitting the high torque of the 4.1 litre Nash engine. With its rapid positive clutch changes, the Laycock overdrive was a great improvement on the slow Borg Warner unit. The first race was the Mille Miglia with the sole Nash Healey driven by the American John Fitch and Warwick mechanic Ray Willday. When the engine was started to warm it up for the start of the race, the Carter carburettors back-fired and ignited. John Fitch just sat there, drawling 'Get a fire extinguisher – somebody get a fire extinguisher.' He was quickly persuaded to open the throttle and the flames were sucked in, putting out the embryo fire. John Fitch did not get far before the crown wheel and pinion in the axle started to howl and the axle failed. Nash had seen this happen before with new hypoid gears, due to lubrication failure. They later came up with an oil incorporat-ing special additives for running-in purposes.

The Nash Healey Specials

At the 1953 Le Mans, our number one pair were Leslie Johnson and Bert Hadley who finished eleventh overall. The second pair, Frenchmen Pierre Veyron and Ives Giraud Cabantous, suffered low oil pressure due to trouble with the oil pump and had to retire. This race marked the end of the Warwick-built special Nash Healeys.

In all, 506 production Nash Healeys were built, from December 1950 to August 1954. These were the 1951 model 25160 with the all-English body, the 1952 model 25262 with the open Farina body, the 1953 model 25367 with the all-steel closed body, and the 1954 model 25367 with the longer wheelbase and revised body. By the time production ceased, the Nash Healey was an expensive car, with a port of entry price of $5,128.

Perhaps the best remembered feature of the Nash Healey was that slow turning high torque engine that would go anywhere in top gear. I also have particularly vivid memories of the coupé with its 1,000-mile cruising range on a 40-gallon tank.

The scheme for the last Nash Healey race cars. The lamp and wing treatment was carried out to try to get lots of air to the front brakes.

After the Show:
The First Twenty

The turning point in Healey fortunes came with the agreement between Len Lord and DMH at the 1952 International Motor Show, whereby Austin undertook the production and marketing of the Healey Hundred as the Austin Healey 100. The International Motor Show, organized by the Society of Motor Manufacturers and Traders and then held annually at London's Earls Court, was and still is the most important motor exhibition in the world. The public saw only the stands and the offices on the show floor, but in the cavernous depths of Earls Court were the offices of all the big manufacturers, where a great deal of hard work was accomplished. For publicity purposes, the hand-shaking and public confirmation of the agreement took place on the Healey stand, but throughout the show, meetings took place in the secluded offices of the Austin Motor Company. It was here that Len Lord and DMH laid down the bare bones of how to effect the agreement.

I had many meetings with the engineering staff of Austin to determine how we could best get the project rolling. Geoff Cooper was to remain our liaison man with the design department of Austin. Fortunately, Geoff had the familiar background of being trained as an apprentice at Austin. He knew every part of a motor car and how and where it was produced. We had worked together to produce the prototype and this partnership would continue throughout the life of the Austin Healey marque.

We were also fortunate in that Austin had one of the great men of the motor industry, J R (Joe) Edwards, in control of day to day matters as a local director. (George Harriman was at that time deputy managing director.) Joe was to chair most of the early meetings and keep things on course. All of us attending these meetings were very busy people, and it was great to be able to sit down and deal with matters swiftly, accurately and efficiently, with a minimum of waffle. Action followed immediately, with the minutes of the meetings invariably arriving in the next post.

As Austin could not start production until the middle of 1953, it was arranged that we would build the first cars at Warwick. Initially, it was laid down that there would be 50 of these pre-production cars, but the change-over from Warwick to Austin production was later to be set for car number 21.* In addition, we would be involved in a competition programme to help promote sales of a car that would be aimed primarily at the American market.

The work load imposed on us at our small Warwick factory was colossal. In a very short space of time, we had to modify aspects of the design and detail drawings for production in what were for us large quantities. We had less than five months in which to produce four pre-production Austin Healey 100s, three for the USA and one for the Geneva show. We also had to produce four competition 100s – two for racing, one spare, and one for record-breaking at Bonneville Salt Flats – and two competition Nash Healeys. We would run the two Nash Healeys and two Austin Healeys in the Mille Miglia in April and in the 24 Hours Race at Le Mans. At the same time, we would remain heavily involved with the day to day production and updating of the Nash Healey and Healey cars, and the 1953 motor shows.

We knew from the start that DMH's engineering team would be hard-pressed to fulfil these demands. Since DMH would be spending most of his time formulating plans for future activities, the brunt of the work would fall on Roger Menadue, who ran the experimental shop. Roger was essentially methodical, refusing to spring into instant action but instead pondering over problems and still managing to produce the perfect solution in a very short time. Like many other experimental mechanics, he was an extremely competent driver, quicker and better than many of the racing drivers we used. He and I were good friends with many interests in common, such as fishing. Such men are invaluable in any small, tightly knit organization.

All the chassis work would be Barry Bilbie's responsibility. Barry had served an apprenticeship with Maudsley, a commercial vehicle manufac-

---

*The chassis numbers of these 20 cars have often caused confusion in the past. They were issued by Austin, and ranged from 133234 to 134379, with many gaps in between. They thus preceded those of the Austin-built cars, which started at 138031.

The first Austin Healey, identified by the small distance between the side- and headlamps. On the cars that followed the headlamp height was increased. (Edward Eves)

turer, and was an extremely fine draughtsman. He was the complete exception to the general rule of draughtsmen who have little or no practical experience, and tend to produce drawings of parts that look beautiful but are the very devil to make and use metal wastefully.

Gerry Coker would handle all the bodywork, raising the front wing line and headlamps, to comply with American regulations, and generally refining details. Like the rest of the team, Gerry had learnt automobile engineering the hard way, in his case through an apprenticeship with the Rootes Group. He had a flair for styling and an eye for line that has been equalled by few in the world's motor industry. He was very quick and the

Austin Healey 100 lines he developed have rarely been bettered by any of the better known stylists. Gerry had another advantage in that he had practical ability: what he drew could be made and would work.

We were fortunate in having as works manager Harry Brandish, who had run the machine shops at Triumph before the war. Harry had an in-depth knowledge of machining problems and we leant heavily on his knowledge and experience to produce drawings of parts that could be made economically. As works manager, Harry was responsible for discipline in the plant. He commanded a great deal of respect and he kept people on the rails without any bullying or nastiness. I cannot forget rushing into his office one day and saying, 'The Old Man wants the shop cleaned up.' Harry bristled and lowered his head to look at me over his spectacles. He then proceeded to admonish me in a few words for using the term 'Old Man'. He gave me a choice of names which he considered more suitable and so I settled for DMH.

Responsibility for purchasing was under the control of Bob Boardman who had worked for DMH at HM Hobson, the aircraft carburettor manufacturers. Bob had the ability to obtain parts and materials during a time of great shortage, at the right prices. During a discussion with Austin it was discovered that we were buying some parts more cheaply than they were, despite a vast difference in volume. Fred Draper ran the stores where he was able to gain a knowledge of Austin Healey parts that would later help him in his business of supplying spares to owners. Fred later took over control of buying, when Bob had to retire due to ill health.

Gerry Coker's original styling drawing for the 100. The air scoop on the bonnet was eliminated, and the fold-flat screen was replaced by the ingenious mechanism devised by Gerry. DMH had the fins removed during production of the prototype body.

The factory at Warwick was always referred to as 'The Works'. After the war, a for once enlightened Warwick Council made land available for factory premises. DMH arranged the purchase of just under 3 acres of reclaimed land in the Cape area. This area was bordered on one side by the Grand Union Canal, with the Cape of Good Hope public house on the water's edge. At that time wartime aircraft hangars were available at reasonable prices and the main building consisted of one of these, with its corrugated iron sheeting erected on a concrete raft. Offices were constructed along one side and at the front, and the material and parts stores along the other side. Later a further raft was laid down and a brick-built factory building erected. In 1953 this building housed the experimental department and it was here that Roger Menadue and his men would build the first pre-production Austin Healeys and the Special Test cars. The Cape factory had plenty of waste land for vehicle storage plus a couple of sheds. The bulk of the hangar was used for the assembly of Healey and Nash Healey chassis and for Geoff Price's service workshop. Areas were reallocated to different use as needs demanded and Roger's experimental shop moved several times.

The hours of work were pretty flexible. The experimental shop worked from 8 am to 7 pm most weekdays, occasionally all day Saturday, normally Saturday mornings and sometimes on Sunday. DMH and I went in most Sunday mornings to review the previous week's achievements and to plan the next week's activities. This was a particularly good time to review things in a quiet deserted factory, free from normal interruptions, and as DMH was spending a great deal of time away from Warwick it was also convenient. In 1953 DMH spent some 90 days overseas on Austin Healey business, mostly in the USA. I probably saw more of him at home in Leamington when we would spend most of the time talking about the cars and work.

The first 20 cars were built at Warwick from parts supplied by Austin and with finished bodies from Jensen Motors. The first three cars were the left-hand-drive models for the USA. They had to be finished, tested and shipped to Austin of America by March 1953. These cars would be the spearhead of a very large number of Austin Healey's to be sent over during the next 17 years. Two cars would be for show, publicity and road test by journalists, and the third would be driven around the USA by DMH. The records of these cars remain in the possession of the family and act as a stimulant to the memory in producing the true story.

The first body came from Jensen in January in an incomplete state, due to a hold up with some bought-out parts. In fact, the first three cars had to be returned to Jensen for various bits to be fitted, once we had completed the build and road tested them. These shortages included the alloy kick plates around the door apertures, the boot, carpeting, cockpit mouldings and some small plated parts. Each of the early cars had a Jensen body number and each moulding was fitted and numbered before being despatched to a plater for polishing.

Whilst the build-up of the cars proceeded, further development work was proceeding on the original show car. Austin wanted to replace the 10 inch diameter drum brakes with the 11 inch ones currently in use on the Austin A70. We gladly accepted this improvement and a series of tests was completed on the prototype using a variety of linings. After each set of linings had been bedded in for a minimum of 500 miles, they were tested for deceleration against pedal effort, fade recovery and after-fade deceleration. They were also subjected to 25 decelerations from 80 mph at one minute intervals, followed by a break of ten minutes and then a further 25 decelerations. Mintex M20 gave by far the best performance under all tests and this confirmed our choice of this material. We had a great deal of experience with this lining, as it had proved to be the only one that would stand up to racing conditions with constant reliability. (Whilst I was wading

100 cockpit showing the overdrive switch mounted on the steering wheel spokes. Many positions for the switch were assessed during the course of development.

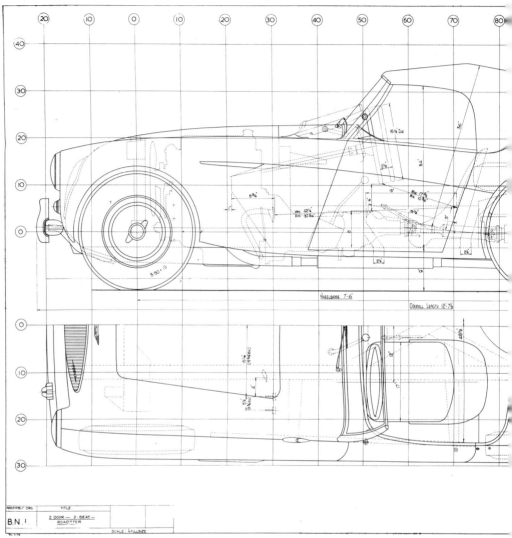

An accurate tracing of the Austin Healey 100, produced at an early stage for publicity and literature purposes. We had not finalized the exhaust system, and this drawing shows a fish tail on the end of the exhaust pipe. This was proved to lose power and was never fitted on production cars.

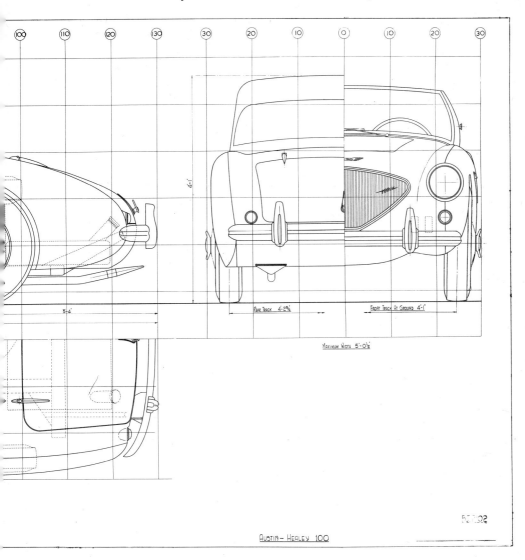

Rear Track 4'-2¾"

Front Track At Ground 4'-1"

Maximum Width 5'-0½"

AUSTIN — HEALEY 100

67

through these brake test figures, I was interested to discover that one of the first 20 cars, 134376, was still being used for brake test work at the close of 1954.) One less fortunate result of the brake changes was that brake fluid got on the paint of the first cars whilst they were under construction, and they had to be repainted.

The overdrive was the subject of constant development, with the aim of improving its life and change quality. Auto Transmissions of Coventry were responsible for the design and development of the unit and Ian Duncan, their chief engineer, was able to make some improvements. The early units had a very harsh take-up under light throttle conditions and the problem was to make this smoother whilst avoiding slip and flare up under full throttle. One feature of the Laycock de Normanville overdrive was this ability to change up under full throttle, in contrast to the Borg Warner unit which could only be changed up on a trailing throttle.

The Laycock unit included cone clutches lined with Minex Halo, a brake lining material used by Bentley for their Le Mans victories. A very slow change with prolonged slip would burn the oil on the surface of the lining, with a resultant drastic reduction in its co-efficient of friction. A clutch that suffered in this way would slip badly. The speed of the change was controlled by a hydraulic accumulator, consisting of a piston and spring operating in a bore in the body of the overdrive. The prototype units had large bore pistons and strong springs, and were very fierce in operation. At this time Laycock came up with the 'baby' accumulator, using a cylinder liner in the bore and a smaller piston.

The car designated for DMH's use when touring America had no less than three overdrive units fitted, plus several spring changes, before were were satisfied. This gave rise to trouble during the tour, when the bolts securing the front of the propeller shaft to the overdrive came loose. The nuts were of the self-locking type and unable to take the strain of being used more than once.

These 20 cars were panelled in aluminium alloy, as this was the quickest way Jensen could produce the panels without proper tooling. As a result, the cars were a few pounds lighter than later production cars and did not suffer corrosion to the same degree. When the first cars arrived in the USA, their boot (trunk) and bonnets (hoods) were found to be dented, due to handling by dockers. For line production Austin introduced steel skins for these items and for the wings and doors. The change from 0.048 inch thick aluminium to 0.036 inch thick steel for the bonnet, the last item to be made in steel, was agreed on 12th October 1953. We had previously tried various stiffening pieces on the bonnet as we wished to retain the light weight of the aluminium to make it easier for owners to lift, but we were unable to defeat the denting problem.

Horses were a normal feature of Austin publicity photos. The 100 looks sleek alongside an Austin Convertible.

One of the first three Austin Healeys, used by DMH on his tour of the USA, and photographed at Sebring in 1953. This car still survives and is being restored in the USA.

Sebring 1953. Mari Hulman, daughter of the owner of Indianapolis Speedway, with DMH and the car DMH used on his sales tour of the USA.

Our Warwick blacksmith, Jack Merralls, hand forged quite a large number of the steering levers before the dies were completed and proper drop forgings became available. The early splined hubs were made from hand forgings which we machined at Warwick, while the splining operation was carried out by Alford and Alder. Douglas at Bristol later made a batch although the final production quantities were scheduled to come from the James Cycle Company.

Gerry Coker spent a lot of time sorting out problems at Jensen, caused mainly by their tendency to cheapen details which would have downgraded the product. Jensen's idea of what a sports car should be was enshrined in one of their prototypes, which was powered by the 1200 cc Austin A40 sports engine. Apart from being nicely finished, it was horrible. Every time we had a meeting with Austin people at the Jensen works, we were always amused to see this thing parked in a prominent position.

On 18th February, Harry Ladd of Armstrong and I did a few runs around the Warwickshire roads to finalize the shock-absorber settings. In a few hours we established settings that were to last throughout the whole BN1 and BN2 production runs, and were continued on the BN4 six cylinders with only increased low speed or leak setting on the front dampers.

Early in February the first three cars were complete and DMH, Roger and I took them out for testing. I drove DMH's tour car to Cornwall and back over a weekend, suffering probems with the overdrive unit. On return to Warwick this was changed and the car driven to Austin for shipment to New York.

These first three cars were shipped in February to cover the Miami World Fair, the New York International Motor Sports Fair, held in Grand Central Palace, and DMH's promotional tour. DMH wrote long letters from the USA, giving detailed reports of defects to be cured and making suggestions for improvements. The USA was to be the main market for Austin Healey cars and so any such defect was carefully investigated and corrected if at all possible. Many of the comments are familiar, including our old friend water-leaks. These were reduced over the years but can still present a problem to owners today. Jensen Motors had been given the job of eliminating these leaks but they tended to skimp on any improvement that might have eaten into their small profit. Whilst DMH was on tour, a rear shock absorber bracket broke away from the frame at 5,000 miles and the rear springs settled by nearly one inch. A simple strengthening plate and an alteration to the shock absorber link length eliminated this fault. As mentioned earlier, the propeller shaft bolts at the rear of the overdrive also came loose.

In addition to this feedback from DMH, the Austin Motor Company Ltd (England), who handled the import of all Austin cars, sent us frequent reports on the cars. Austin of England, as they proudly called themselves, had a number of practical service men operating throughout North America. These men were mainly ex-factory employees, many of whom had served their time at Longbridge as apprentices. They had had a rough time sorting out problems with Austin's earlier imports, such as the A40 Devon and Dorset models, and were well aware of the dangers of a repeat of these troubles with the Austin Healey. The files are full of reports from men such as Andy Woods, Peter Millard, Ken Harris, Cyril Fowler, Mike Barratt, Graham Gardner, Brian Green, Jack Ryan and Eric Vale – just a few of those who helped improve the Austin Healey for the American market.

The meeting in Joe Edward's office on 23rd March considered a number of these problems. Joe was not able to chair the meeting and the minutes make somewhat odd reading, including: '2: Mr Healey expressed his non-

A line of 100s ready for competition, in 1954.

approval of the wiring scheme as laid down by Austin Chassis Drawing Office. It was arranged that this matter will be the subject of discussion between Mr Richardson of Austin Drawing Office and Mr Healey.' The point under discussion was our refusal to accept cars with the main wiring loom drooping below the main chassis members!

These minutes also recorded the position at that time: five cars completed, two nearing completion, three in paint at Jensens, and five more in the early stages of body assembly. With the first five cars completed and most of the assembly problems sorted out, it was now possible to pass the remainder of the relatively simple assembly work over to the production workshop at Warwick, run by Harry Brandish, assisted by Reg Muir and Geoff Price. It was now necessary for Roger's experimental shop to concentrate on the Austin Healey Special Test cars and the Nash Healey racing cars.

72

DMH photographing the 1953 Austin Healey.

A scheme for a conventional drop head coupé on the 100. This car was built and the top conversion was carried out by Tickfords.

The Special Test Cars

Large motor manufacturers do not lightly become involved in racing for a number of good reasons. Any failure reflects badly on the engineering competence of the manufacturer, while victory tends to be dismissed as the inevitable result of the marshalling of vast resources. Additionally, a competition programme places greater loads on engineering, experimental and development departments which are generally overloaded, undermanned and behind in fulfilment of their normal function of producing new models. One can contrast the success of Ford and Jaguar when they decided to go out and win, with the failure of the French giant Renault who have achieved meagre success in competition with the relatively small companies racing today.

Like so many large manufacturers, Austin wanted the publicity benefits of competition and racing whilst remaining outwardly uncommitted. To disguise this interest, they decided that competition vehicles would be designated Special Test Cars. Len Lord and DMH had agreed the bare bones of the competition programme, leaving the implementation of it to Geoff Cooper and myself. Four cars were to be built, two for racing plus one spare, and one for record breaking.

Once the policy and programme had been determined, it was then necessary to have some numbers to book the work and the cars against. Austin issued us with order numbers covering the work and specific numbers for the cars – ST 224, 5 and 6 for the competition cars, and ST 227 for the record car. They also supplied us with their chassis plates, with the numbers SPL 224 B to SPL 227 B. In addition we issued work numbers AHR 5–8 to cover our work at Warwick, plus some X marks to cover specific events and record breaking. This enabled separate costs to be allocated to cars, events and ancillary items. Even in a small organization like ours, it was important to maintain accurate records of costs if we were to keep within budget figures. It was also necessary to keep others outside the engineering division from getting into the act and using our numbers to book unrelated work.

Although our small team at Warwick was fully committed with the engineering of the production vehicles and the construction of the 20 pre-production vehicles, we had to fit in the construction of the four special cars and organizing their campaigns. At this time the engineering team consisted of Roger Menadue, experimental engineer, Gerry Coker on body design, Barry Bilbie on chassis design and a couple of boys in the drawing office. It was Roger who had to carry out the construction of the cars, despite constant interruption from the service and production crew who were building 2.4 litre Healeys and Nash Healeys in the main shop.

An Austin publicity photograph: Miss Hazel Cleaver of Birmingham – Miss Britain – with the Austin Healey 100. The car's UK price was then £750 plus £313.12s.6d. purchase tax.

75

It would be wrong to try to convey that all was harmony and sweetness. Because he was a friend of the family, Roger came in for a lot of petty jealousy from certain members of our team, whom we privately christened the 'thickoes'. They used to complain frequently about some of his activities or apparent lack of activity and in retrospect it seems that there was a continuous campaign to get Roger out. Roger had the knack of being both ingenious and irritating by getting the job done without any struggle or apparent effort. Number one thicko would creep into me and moan that Roger had not started on the car and had gone off to some scrap yard. Number two thicko would then be in to tell me that Roger was painting a 'foreigner' in some corner of the works. (A 'foreigner' is something used for some purpose unrelated to the firm's business.) Later thickoes would return to complain some more, by which time I would be delighted to inform them that by using a device fabricated and painted by Roger we had been able to complete the work on the car in a fraction of normal time, and furthermore that we now had a device costing next to nothing that would enable any repeat procedure to be effected speedily and at little cost. In fact, I don't think that the thickoes really understood engineering and they would merely slink away to sharpen up their dull wits for a future assault. The best fitters and mechanics do not appear to leap into action, reducing everything to a heap of bits in a short time; they think and complete the job with precision and disguised speed. This is a digression from the nitty-gritty story of the specials, but it is useful to understand some of the pressures under which the work of building the cars took place.

We had a further problem with Len Lord's minions, when it came to translating decisions made by him and DMH at meetings at which minutes were not kept. Without an internal order number, nothing could happen at Austin, and absolutely no one at Austin would dare ask Len Lord what had been agreed as they would then have been blasted for not having acted. It was one of Geoff Cooper's functions to keep us in touch with events at Austin, and somehow he and I managed to turn high-up decisions into order numbers and action. Much of the time, Geoff would act at great personal risk as the result of a 'phone call from me, outlining the decisions of the great. Geoff, an ex-Austin apprentice, had a knowledge of Austin units that was second to none, backed up by a fantastic memory of parts that would be useful. He would often sit down with me in my office, a draughty corner under the eaves of the main hangar, heated with some difficulty by a coal-burning stove, and draw up specifications and schedules of what we could use from Austin.

The limitations imposed on us were that the cars should look like the production model and utilize readily obtainable Austin components. An order was given to Jensen Motors to complete four bodies on chassis frames supplied by John Thompson of Wolverhampton, using panels formed in Birmabright. This is an aluminium alloy produced by a company of that name located at Quinton in Birmingham. BB3, the alloy used on our bodies, contained 3 per cent of magnesium which resulted in the best corrosion resistance allied to an ultimate tensile strength of 17 to 19 tons per square inch. (It should not be confused with magnesium alloys, which will burn readily and constitute a fire hazard.) Bodies built in this alloy are strong, light and strongly resistant to corrosion, and for these reasons they are to be found on Land Rovers and many boats. Anyone owning a Healey constructed with one of these alloys is fortunate, as it will endure. The bodies were to be finished in a metallic paint supplied by Dockers. We used green, the traditional British racing colour, though not in the traditional shade of British Racing Green. The paint process used specially formulated etching primers which resulted in a far superior paint adhesion to that on the production vehicles. Seats trimmed in green leather from Conolly's with a green Everflex trim from Bernard Wardle completed the job.

The power units were the responsibility of Austin's engine men, Bill Appleby, Don Hawley and Eric Barham, and were specified to produce in excess of 100 bhp. The crankshaft came from the Austin Champ and was made in an EN40, a high tensile nitriding steel. Nitriding is a process in which a finished article made in a special alloy steel is exposed to an atmosphere of ammonia gas at a temperature of about 500°C for a predetermined period of time. The special feature of the process is that this temperature does not modify the properties of the material apart from its skin, which is hardened for a depth of a few thousandths of an inch. Crankshafts are finished before being treated in this way, with only small allowances for polishing and other minor operations. The resulting high strength and extreme surface hardness form an ideal combination for long crankshaft life. The nitriding process on these crankshafts was carried out by Rolls-Royce.

The only other non-standard parts used in the engines were a camshaft with longer opening periods and more overlap, double valve springs and a lighter flywheel. The experimental department at Austin built these engines with special care, paying particular attention to the clearance between the rear oil scroll of the crankshaft and its housing. This type of oil sealing arrangement was known to be suspect on the Austin engine and liable to give trouble at high engine speeds. In this form the engines produced around 100 bhp at 4,500 rpm and were to prove very reliable.

We were also aware that the gearbox would have a very small margin of safety and could have been the weak link in long distance races. At this time, Austin were making a four-speed gearbox with wider shaft centres for the London taxis that withstood the most diabolical treatment by the worst

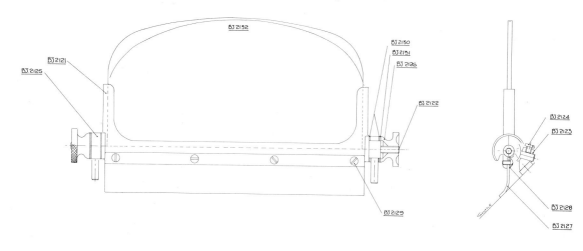

AERO SCREEN ASSY BJ 2120

A drawing of the optional aero screen on the 100. These were easily fitted to the scuttle and the rubber seal kept some water off the driver.

cab drivers for over 100,000 miles. The ratios were far from ideal, but some changes to the gears resulted in a box which when coupled to the Laycock de Normanville gearbox gave seven speeds – first, second, overdrive second, third, overdrive third, top and overdrive top. In practice overdrive second proved too much for the overdrive and was not used. The poor shift qualities of this gearbox were more than compensated for by the excellent ratios and reliability.

Clutch design had not advanced greatly since the end of the war and the special clutch provided by Borg and Beck of Leamington Spa was the weak link in the power train. To be fair to Borg and Beck, I should emphasize that we were working to a very tight programme with little time for development and testing. Jaguar had lost the 1950 Le Mans race when the clutches failed on their XK120s and we made sure that the clutch supplied for the Special Test cars used a different metal centre plate that overcame this weakness. However, this new design did not have a sufficient number of rivets attaching the lining material to the metal centre. These was no sign of any weakness over a considerable test mileage and the first trouble came near the end of the Mille Miglia, when the clutch plate disintegrated. A total of five of these power units was built by Austin for the Special Test cars.

Austin supplied all the normal running gear for the cars while we obtained all the special parts. Wilmott Breedon produced bumper bars in high strength aluminium alloy with a highly polished bright finish. These bumpers saved weight and were not easily distinguishable from their plated steel production counterparts. Perhaps we should have claimed a first in the field and put them on all the cars. The cars of today often use bright aluminium bumpers.

Marston Radiators supplied four radiators of production form but made in aluminium alloy. Although these reduced front end weight, there were reservations about their effective life. Oil companies were not then producing anti-freeze mixtures with suitable inhibitors to prevent corrosion and build-up of deposits. In practice, these alloy radiators exceeded the manufacturer's projected life, most being scrapped due to collision damage. One outlived several cars before it was finally scrapped due to build up of deposits in the tubes.

The production brakes supplied by Girling would need considerable improvement if they were to stand up to the long distance endurance races for which the cars were being developed. On the 1952 Nash Healey race cars we had used their $11 \times 2\frac{1}{4}$ twin trailing shoe front brakes. Without the servo action of twin leading shoe brakes, these were very stable and resistant to fade, and had self-adjusting shoes. We considered that they should be capable of consistent performance without requiring any time-consuming adjustment throughout a 24 hour race. Girling provided competent technical back-up with reliable data and installation information. The production commitment with Austin meant that installation would be the responsibility of Girling's second-to-none installation department run by George Wood. We would have liked to use light alloy Al-Fin brake drums to save on unsprung weight but in the light of previous experience we were worried that we might run into liner cracking in an endurance race. There is never enough time to assess all one's options thoroughly, and so we settled for the devil we knew, cast iron drums. We would lose a bit on handling with the increased unsprung weight but reliability is always the paramount consideration when racing a new car. The linings were Mintex M20 which would stand more punishment than the finest drums and were standard fitments on the production Austin Healey. Girling's resident installation engineer at Austin, Ken Light, was responsible for all the hosing, piping and installation, so we had no worries in that respect. In practice, pedal effort – the amount of push the driver has to put on the brake pedal – was high. This would have been unacceptable for normal vehicle use but presented no problems to the racing drivers of that era.

When construction was well under way at Warwick, Austin asked us if we could finish one car in time to use it for demonstration purposes at the Geneva Show in March. We agreed to do this gladly: it would mean working long hours, but the chance to test the car on the Continent prior to the Mille Miglia, and at someone else's expense, was too good to miss. Roger of course had the car completed on time and a brief test on our Warwickshire roads was all that was required to confirm that everything was functioning as it should. During the initial running in, we never applied the brakes hard from speed, instead applying them lightly and often to speed up the bedding in process. In this way, we avoided heat spotting the drums which would have led to surface cracks on their braking surfaces and to judder and rapid lining wear. Those first few miles are very important and can affect the future performance of the car. Of course, one would scan the gauges almost as often as the road, but in the main reliance would be placed on one's other senses. One would feel through the floor, through the seat and through the controls; one's ears would pick up the slightest change of sound and one's nose any abnormal scent. In this way the car could be run up to full performance safely and in a very short time.

Not many people drove the Special Test cars on the road when they were in their prime, and only a handful of racing drivers, DMH, Mort Goodall, Roger and myself really got to grips with them. The first car, SPL 224B, registered NOJ 391, really was something special. With taut, firm suspension, it projected a feeling of responsive performance waiting to be unleashed. It is difficult to describe the exhilaration you feel with the first run of a new car which you have seen right through from a few bits of paper to a living machine. It is something I have experienced many times, each subtly different but always invigorating and inspiring.

Cecil Winby borrowed NOJ 392 after Le Mans and took part in the Bugatti Owners Club Hill Climb at Prestcott in September 1953. This was believed to be the first appearance of the Austin Healey in competition in the UK.

Back at the works, I checked the car over with Roger, making notes on any points that needed attention and on any improvements that could be incorporated into the two sister cars nearing completion. There was plenty of work for the experimental department – the remaining Special Test cars, the two Nash Healey race cars and the remainder of the first 20 pre-Austin-production Austin Healeys. I then packed a bag and left Warwick to catch the night ferry from Dover to Dunkirk. At around 6 in the morning it was possible to cruise for hours at 90 mph across the flat portion of northern France. Though firm, the ride was not uncomfortable and the car was not in the least bit tiring to drive. In the hilly regions approaching Switzerland, I was able to sample the advantages of seven speeds in the gearbox while keeping the engine turning over at the top end of the power band. When conditions allowed, it was possible to climb in overdrive third, switching down to direct third for the bends and up to overdrive for the straight. This resulted in very rapid progress.

The gear change of the taxi box was heavy and slow, occupying both hands and feet for a rapid change up from an overdrive gear to a high direct ratio. Over the following years, we tried a variety of switch combinations to try to improve this system – switches on the spokes of the steering wheel, stalk switches on the gearbox tunnel and switches built into the gearchange lever knob. The latter had the best action although the early ones tended to fail due to vibration. We found that using the clutch for all changes was an advantage, as it reduced loads on the overdrive clutches and eliminated the chance of a tired driver trying to change gear without using the clutch. Today, after a long period of development, Lucas produce robust small switches for the gear knob position.

I arrived at Geneva with a very short list of work that would need to be carried out. This I sent back to Warwick so that Roger would have everything ready for my return and would be able to modify the remaining Special Test cars. The car attracted tremendous attention as it was the first Austin Healey ever seen on the road in Europe.

Austin had a queue of journalists and Swiss distributors lined up to try the car over the rest of the week. Robert Braunsweig, editor of Europe's top motoring publication, *Automobile Review*, had Switzerland's top racing driver, Willy Daetwyler, on hand. Willy gave the car a short work-out and spoke highly of its performance, although he expressed some reservations about the degree of damping provided by the shock absorbers.

During lunch on the first day, Austin's European representative asked me where I was staying. When I told him, he exclaimed: 'That's a brothel – you can't stay there!' I had seen no signs of anything unusual: I had a large comfortable room at very low cost and was quite happy. However, he insisted that I move to their prestigious hotel where my room was much

Lita Sampietro and Margot relaxing with DMH at St Moritz.

smaller, very dark, and very, very expensive. Of course, appearances count for much when selling cars overseas and even the poorest companies try to create an air of prosperity.

I spent the next few days in the mountains with Margot, who was working as a Thomas Cook representative at a ski resort. This enabled me to try the car on more hill climbs, some with and some without snow.

When I returned to England, the car had covered 3,000 miles and was ready for a partial strip and critical examination. Of course, it leaked water: prior to the 3000 convertible, with years of development behind it, all our good cars leaked. By this time NOJ 392 was ready for test. This was identical to 391: there was no way one could tell them apart. I continued to run 391 and Roger 392, much to the annoyance of the thickoes who looked on the development of motor cars as unnecessary joyriding. It was fun but it was also essential!

Gregor Grant of *Autosport* was probably the first person to rally an Austin Healey, taking one on the Lyons-Charbonnières Rally in March with Peter Reece. He used one of the early pre-production cars and suffered a number of troubles which resulted in a low overall position.

Gregor was persuaded by Ferodo experts to fit their bonded NE99 lining. Just why he should want to replace the tried and reliable Mintex M20 is not known. He complained to us that 'Bad fading and overheating of the drum was experienced in the Alpine sections. When the drums cooled down, braking reappeared, but grabbing, snatching and locking on were experienced.'

The first serious event to be entered by 391 and 392 was the Mille Miglia Road Race in Italy. We had achieved very good results in this race with Healey and Nash Healey cars. The two cars were ideal for the road conditions of the Mille Miglia course and should have done well. The experienced Austin racing driver Bert Hadley had Squadron Leader Bertie Mercer as his co-driver, while ex-racing motor cyclist Johnny Lockett was paired with Jock Reid, who was second to Roger in the experimental shop. Both cars suffered throttle linkage failure. Jock Reid was able to fix the linkage on 391 but the car fell by the wayside 100 miles from the finish, when well placed, with clutch failure caused by the break-up of the plate. It was disappointing but nevertheless we had gained valuable competition experience with the new cars and were able to take action to prevent the same faults recurring in later events.

For Le Mans, NOJ 393 and 392 were our official entry, with the older 391 as a practice car. I am not certain which cars were in fact used as like all other competition departments we did tend to swap the numbers about. The two cars selected for the race had more up to date equipment, including Timken taper roller bearing front hubs. Their engines were measured and stamped by the RAC, while the Le Mans scrutineers took a record of their chassis numbers. Unfortunately, when one of our drivers, Gordon Wilkins of *Autocar*, was driving one of the cars back from scrutineering after lunch, he was struck by a semi-comitose French lorry driver who proceeded out of a side road without any warning. The Le Mans organizers insisted that we could not run our spare car in its place and so all the appropriate parts had to be transferred to NOJ 391. Our team was by then in a sorry state, thanks to a virulent French stomach bug, and this rebuilding work was carried out by Roger, myself and whichever of the mechanics could risk any distance between himself and the nearest lavatory. The rebuilt car was driven by Gordon Wilkins of the *Autocar* and Marcel Becquart, an experienced French racing and rally driver. A sticking overdrive slowed them up considerably and they finished in 14th place overall. Johnny Lockett and Maurice Gastonides in the second car finished 12th overall and second in class.

The report that follows is taken unaltered from the files and gives some factual detail on 391.

NOJ 391

This car was built and used in England prior to Le Mans. The car covered about 2,000 miles before arriving at Le Mans. It then did several practice runs.

Following the crash of the one race car, the engine and gearbox of the race car together with the Timken front hubs were fitted to this car for the race. A new overdrive of .778 ratio was fitted.

In the race the car covered about 2,160 miles. After the race the car was checked over, oil changed and the best available front brake linings and drums were fitted. The car was then used for 2,000 miles including high speed ascents and descents of the Gotthard Pass and high speeds for prolonged periods on Autostrada. On the car one rear axle oil seal and paper washer were replaced.

The oils used were:–
    Engine   – Shell X100 SAE 30
    Gearbox   – Shell X100 SAE 40 with anti-foaming additive
    Rear Axle – Shell Spirax 90 E.P.

Engine of Car NOJ 391

This engine was fitted as received from The Austin Motor Company. It covered 4,000 miles of Continental testing including passes and Autostrada.

It was then used in the Mille Miglia covering 900 miles of the Race at which stage the clutch plate failed. A replacement plate was made up on the spot and the car returned to England. Running to and from the race account for 2,000 miles.

The engine was then prepared for Le Mans. The special camshaft valve springs and carburettors (H.6) were fitted. At the same time the sump capacity was increased and an oil temperature gauge added. When fitting the camshaft pitting of the tappets was noticed. Standard tappets were obtained and these were treated by British Piston Ring Company. At the same time the gearbox was modified by adding an additional breather, a drain in the nose piece, three ventilation holes in the bell housing and a gauze covered one at the top. A special crimped arcuate solid centre clutch plate lined with Mintex M.19 was fitted. The gear lever action was eased by stoning the selector detents. After re-assembly the car was tested on a long runway.

The Race NOJ 391

The car was driven in the race by Marcel Becquart and Gordon Wilkins. The drivers were instructed not to exceed 4,500 rpm.

At about the third hour the overdrive stuck in overdrive. The drivers were therefore instructed to leave it in the overdrive position and to use the gearbox. At the third hour engine and gearbox oils were checked and found satisfactory.

At six-and-half hours a further check was made and all was satisfactory.

At about ten hours a further check was made and a little oil – about ½ pint – was added to the gearbox.

At about thirteen hours the drivers came in and reported miss-firing. All plugs were changed and about 1½ pints of oil were added to the engine. Two of the plugs were clean but did not look as if they had been firing properly.

At about sixteen hours the driver again reported miss-firing. The plugs were examined and the best four of the eight fitted. Oils were checked and found satisfactory.

At about nineteen hours again miss-firing was reported. Quick reference to the Lap Charts showed that the car started miss-firing at about thirty-four laps each time. It was assumed that the fuel was low enough to uncover the end of the main suction pipe during cornering resulting in fuel starvation. A plug switch was made and oil was added to the engine – about $1\frac{1}{2}$ pints – and to the gearbox – $\frac{1}{2}$ pint. The water was checked and found to be satisfactory. The right-hand front wheel was changed on Dunlop's advice. It was decided that the car should be called in before thirty-four laps and risk of miss-firing arose.

At about twenty-three-and-half hours the car was called in and re-fuelled.

The car ran through to the end without trouble.

At the end of the race the clutch was slipping, this was probably due to getting away in overdrive. The miss-firing was found to be due to the burring over of the overflow pipe end from the rear float chamber. This pipe had touched the engine at the end and the vibration had burred and completely blocked the end resulting in complete sealing of the float chamber. It is assumed that the low fuel level caused air to build up in the float chamber resulting in a lock and straight through fuel flow.

The fuel consumption was calculated to be in the region of 18 mpg. Oil used in the engine about 4 pints, in the gearbox about $1\frac{1}{2}$ pints.

A very careful checking of oils and car was made at pit stops as we had no experience of racing this engine in this race and we were intent on collecting data for future races.

The oil temperature during the race reached a maximum of 210°F. The water temperature ran between 65° and 75°C. The oil pressure was consistently 55/60 lbs per sq in.

One reserve driver during practice put in some very fast laps and the oil temperature rose to 225°F.

Some engine oil was obviously lost through the rocker cover gasket. This gasket seems to age with heat causing a leak.

The car ran on Dunlop R1 Racing tyres – 6.00×15 rear at 33 lb per sq in and 5.50×15 front at 30 lbs per sq in.

Conclusions

The car in its present form could go much faster if the permitted rpm were increased. However, oil temperature rises with rpm as does oil consumption. At over 5,000 there is smell of blowby.

The brakes need improving for racing.

Gearbox oil loss is serious as it appears that a certain amount reaches the clutch. The availability of five ratios is a great advantage. An improved gear change would help.

The engine is a very good unit for which all drivers have nothing but praise.

The car was easily the most standard of all cars running.

After the race we checked the car over and changed the oil, and I then took it off to Italy for a few days with Margot.

NOJ 391 was next to race in the Goodwood 9 Hour Race in August. It was essentially a long-distance car, not really suited to a short circuit like Goodwood, but with Johnny Lockett and Ken Rudd it finished 10th overall. Ken Rudd had been reserve driver at Le Mans.

Round about the time of the Goodwood race, another car wearing the same NOJ 391 licence plates was being used in record-breaking attempts at Utah. This was the fourth Special Test car, the plates being used to enable it to be driven on the public highways.

Both cars were used by friends like piston expert, Cecil Winby, at Prestcott Hill Climb and other sprint events. At times we were pressurized into lending cars to odd people and NOJ 391 was lent in this way to a Frenchman for the Tour de France. He managed to wreck it almost totally. It was rebuilt with a production body shell and was later converted to a 100 S.

NOJ 392 was fitted with prototype Girling disc brakes and for the rest of its known life acted as a test car and general transport for Roger. It was finally sold with an incredible mileage, when it was burning oil and in need of a major rebuild. No one knows what happened to it subsequently – it may be still running.

NOJ 393 was fitted with Dunlop racing disc brakes and was used for brake development before being converted to a 100 S.

The fourth Special Test car, SPL 227/B, was used for record attempts at Utah and was never registered for road use, although it was occasionally seen under 391 plates. It was later rebodied and fitted with a six-cylinder engine for long distance record attempts, finally being scrapped in 1957.

The Special Test cars had done all that could be expected of them and had backed the sales efforts with a useful competition record.

The First Record Breakers

The original suggestion that we should go after speed records came from Captain GET (George) Eyston, several times holder of the World Land Speed Record and a director of CC Wakefield, the manufacturers of Castrol oil. George, DMH and Len Lord discussed and agreed on a record breaking programme as an expansion of the competition work already in hand. With his vast experience in the field, George undertook to make the arrangements for the attempts. The location was to be the salt flats at Bonneville, Utah, where George had made many successful runs with Thunderbolt, his land speed record holder, and Speed of the Wind, his long distance car. His old rival and friend, Abe Jenkins, was Mayor of Salt Lake City and the Bonneville flats came under his jurisdiction.

While George made all the arrangements in the USA, the construction of a special car was put in hand at the Cape. This, the fourth of the Special Test cars, formed the basis of the non-stock car that would attack International Class 'D' (2,001–3,000 cc) records. The term non-stock was used to differentiate it from the stock car, which would be drawn from US dealers' vehicle stocks. This would be used to break a very large number of US stock car records during the same trip.

George produced a list of the existing Class D records together with the speeds we would need to achieve in order to break them. He wanted us to break the records by the minimum necessary margin, so that we could go again the following year and break our own records, thereby getting the maximum publicity value from the exercise. He also kept feeding in a constant flow of recommendations, concerning features that would be necessary to cope with the conditions under which the car would operate. Some of these were simply not practicable on a small car such as the Healey.

At times the car could be running on wet salt which would subject its understructure to an intense high speed salt spray. George had experienced tightening up or partial seizure of the steering on his Speed of the Wind due to ingress of salt into the king pins and steering parts. In the 1950s, chassis lubrication, including pumping oil into the swivel axles, was a regular service feature every 1,000 miles. We would be running over 3,000 miles in 24 hours and would not want to waste time with a grease gun every 1,000 miles. Instead, we decided to install piped chassis lubrication. Girling dug out some of their pre-war Luvax Bijur equipment. With the aid of small bore, $\frac{1}{8}$-inch copper piping, flexible hoses, various fittings and a pump, a system was built into the car. The small pump was coupled to the clutch pedal, so that every time the clutch was operated a small quantity of Castrol EP140 gear oil would be pumped into the top and bottom swivel axle bearings. If the driver sensed a stiffening of the steering he had only to pump the clutch pedal twice to lubricate the steering. The surplus oil would flow to the underside of the car and help prevent salt encrustation. This system worked very well in practice and we were to experience no problems with stiff steering.

The changes required to make the Special Test car into a record-breaking car were not extensive. DMH and I sat down and drafted out a specification sheet and then consulted with Roger, Barry and Gerry on how best to achieve the results. A few drawings were made by Barry of items like the large fuel tank and Gerry provided a few sketches of the body modifications. The procurement of bought-out items from a variety of suppliers would in the main be the responsibility of Bob Boardman and Fred Draper, acting on precise details provided by us, which included the names of the suppliers. The nomination of suppliers was always an engineering function. Rather than laying down a rigid specification of a part and then leaving the buying department free to negotiate with suppliers and obtain the most favourable prices, we would specify a supplier upon whom we could rely as far as quality was concerned. The buying department would moan and groan about the lack of freedom to select suppliers but I am certain that this policy gave us quality and reliability. Overall there was little in the way of a cost penalty.

The wheels and tyres came from Dunlop who had amassed more experience of high-speed record breaking than any other tyre manufacturer. At that time the only tyres they had available were in 16-inch diameter with many plies. These provided a stiff unyielding carcass with thin treads devoid of any pattern, apart from circumferential grooves to aid checking of tread wear. Heat and centrifugal force are the main obstacles to be overcome during continuous high speed use. The stiff carcass minimizes flexing and the generation of heat, whilst a light tread is less likely to separate from the carcass under high speed operation.

The power unit was the first of the four-port Weslake-designed units hurriedly built and developed by Austin. The responsibility of developing the unit fell to Don Hawley, a brilliant young engineer at Longbridge. He set up the engine for Utah to give 131.5 bhp at 4,750 rpm, running on a 9 to 1 compression ratio and using Esso Extra fuel. The power output was almost identical to what Eddie Maher and Jack Goffin would give us with the production 100 S engines later on.

Harry Weslake designed the heads to fit on a basic cylinder block with a different stud disposition. He moved the inlet and exhaust ports from the left, push-rod side of the engine, to the right. With the traditional Austin design, the push rods restricted the number and size of ports that could be accommodated, whereas on the other side there were only the cylinder head studs to avoid. This meant that the exhaust system ran down the right-hand side of the car, and so we built it with left-hand drive to position the driver on the less hot side of the driving compartment. I use the term less hot advisedly, as in the 90°F (32.22°C for the metricated) ambient temperature that would be encountered in Utah, it would still be warm. A 4-inch flexible duct from the front of the car would blow air to the driver's feet and body, but air at 90°F plus what it picked up when passing through the engine compartment is hardly an effective cooling medium. Three hours under the midday sun at Utah in a hot Healey is better than any sauna in removing excess body weight. (Despite the views expressed by many owners, we were very conscious of the need to keep the floor of cars at reasonable temperatures: it was just that the state of the art of vehicle heat insulation was not very advanced in the 1950s.)

We calculated the fuel tank capacity sufficient to give three hours' endurance at 125 mph and Barry drew up the tank with its large quick action filler cap to fit in the boot (trunk) of the car. Two of SU's LCS pumps forced the fuel to the engine. One would have been sufficient but pumps have been known to fail.

The car was gutted of any surplus material or equipment, including the passenger's seat. The passenger compartment was covered with a light alloy tonneau panel incorporating an air duct to purge hot air from this area. George Perry of Lucas was later to steal some of the cooling air and duct it to the battery to stop it boiling dry.

Roger and his merry men, and they were a great bunch of loyal workers, grafted whatever hours were necessary to meet the completion date. Some

Gaydon airfield, 1953. DMH testing the first S-engined car on what is now British Leyland's test ground.

had been union men during the war but there were no union activists or militants to cause dissension. The car was ready on schedule, with equipment such as a rear view mirror and trade plates added for me to give it a road test. With great care, I gave it a run over our Warwickshire test route. This was more in the nature of a function and systems check than a road test, to confirm that it was suitable for a proper test on a local airfield. I made a few notes of the changes needed and Roger and I then crawled all over the car, looking for possible defects, oil leaks or signs of tyres rubbing on the bodywork. There was little that needed to be done – a result of the high quality of the work. The Air Ministry readily gave us permission to use the runways at the Gaydon RAF base, just 7 miles from Warwick. This airfield has now been converted into one of the country's finest vehicle test facilities by British Leyland, and is thus no longer available to companies outside the group.

DMH and I gave the car a serious test to make sure that it would handle at speed, would reach the specified speed, and that it felt right. It is more the feeling that something is right than sets of test figures that count: there was never any reason to doubt the accuracy of the various necessary calculations or the honesty of Austin's engine output figures.

SPL 227/B was by far the fastest Austin Healey we had tried. With a kerb weight of 1,850 lbs over 130 bhp and a completely unsilenced exhaust system, it would surge away to over 120 mph over the 3,000-yard runway. One did not floor the pedal and scream off with smoke pouring from the rear tyres, for rapid acceleration means little in long-distance record runs. It was far more important to avoid unduly stressing the drive train. For the Sunday morning test runs, Len Lord himself came along to see and check up on the project. Every one was ecstatic over the performance and potential of this, the first record breaker, and felt the satisfaction of a job well done.

The car was to be transported together with a large quantity of spares to Southampton, to be loaded onto one of Cunard's *Queen*s for shipment to New York. DMH and I discussed the car most of that Sunday evening, thinking of the next generation of Special Test cars and already forming ideas for the production of a car with that engine.

Most of the team sailed for New York on a Cunard liner – five days of enforced relaxation. In the early 1950s, Atlantic greyhounds were much more reliable than aircraft. Fred Horner of Austin of England met us in New York and helped us buy some suitable clothing to cope with the August heat wave before putting us on a train for Salt Lake. Over the years, Fred Horner met all the BMC teams and saw them safely out of New York. Today he still retains a great interest in club activities.

From the train we had a view of much of the USA, travelling in great comfort at comparatively slow speed. From Salt Lake City, Austin of England's technical representatives drove us to Wendover on the edge of the salt flats, where George Eyston had set up base at Clarence McLeod's Motel. We had the use of a local garage which would tackle any sort of repair on automobiles. The Austin reps or field service engineers were an excellent bunch, who invariably came to work equipped with wonderful tool kits. We set to and got the cars ready for some test runs.

We hoped that the Castrol clutch-pump system would deal with any attack from salt spray. In addition, we sprayed the underside of the cars with a special oil that would dry to a soft sticky grease and liberally coated critical areas where salt might built up with a Castrol lanolin grease.

The Bonneville salt flats, 4,228 feet above sea level and 120 miles west of Salt Lake City, are one of the wonders of the world. Over millions of years the waters of the lake became progressively more salty until a level surface of rough crystalline material was formed. Usually, although not every year, evaporation and lack of rainfall causes this to be hard and firm. When the Flats are to be used as a high-speed surface, the Utah State Highway Department drags a length of railway line over a straight length of up to 13 miles and around in a circle of 10 miles in diameter. At either end of the straightaway the salt becomes progressively softer until it ends in salt water. One has to be careful not to go too far off the beaten or swept track, or the car will sink out of sight. The test areas are surveyed and marked out with a black oil line. The American Automobile Association's competition division were responsible for the accurate surveying and measuring of the straightaway and circle, and for timing all the record attempts. The AAA's officials normally officiated at the Indianapolis 500 and were lifetime devotees of the sport – ex-racing drivers, ex-mechanics and enthusiasts.

George Eyston had organized everything and once the cars had been well treated with the protective oils, we travelled in convoy from our base to the salt flats. The special car was running on 600×16 and 6.50×16 Dunlop tyres, and 3.65 to 1 rear axle, with the standard production 0.756 to 1 overdrive fitted to the taxi gearbox, giving a speed of 140 mph at just over 4,500 rpm. We arrived ahead of our booked time at the flats when the National Hot Rod Association were in control, but they kindly let us try the car. The mixture setting was not quite right for the high altitude. The water temperature was low and so we blanked off the upper portion of the grille and extended the air intakes through the grille. We carried out a number of small changes, lowering the windscreen, removing the Lucas 'flame thrower' lamps and polishing the body to a high standard. It was encouraging to find that what was basically a production car ran straight and was easily controlled at a speed so far above its designed speed.

By kind permission of the National Hot Rod Association, DMH did a run up the straightaway and was timed by their timers, Southern California Timing Association Inc, at 131.81 mph. This was slower than we had calculated and DMH reported that he was convinced that the engine was

DMH at speed in the first S engined car, on the 10-mile circle at Bonneville salt flats.

Gerry Coker produced this following the 1953 record runs. Neville Duke had just broken the world speed record in a British aircraft. The feet marked R and M belong to Roger Menadue.

misfiring at speed. We checked and reset valve clearance at .015 inch, and set the contact breaker gap and the ignition timing, using static setting with feeler gauges. We checked the fuel pump outputs against a stop watch, and then tried different and richer carburettor needles. The car now accelerated to a higher speed without any sign of misfiring.

On 9th September DMH was officially timed at 142.55 mph for the kilometre and 142.64 mph for the mile. This was the cause of great jubilation as it was the highest speed recorded by a production sports car at that time. It certainly dwarfed the 125 mph obtained by Triumph with the TR2.

Five days later, we took the car out to the 10 mile circle, for the endurance run. The driving was to be shared between DMH, George Eyston, Bill Spear and John Gordon Benett. The car circulated the course at speeds around 125 mph without any real effort. The official AAA timers timed every lap while their eagle-eyed observers, placed around the circle, watched out for any infringements. We took it in turns to signal to the driver, check lap speeds, talk about cars, and eat, making sure that someone was always available for an unscheduled pit stop. We called the car in every three hours for a driver change, refuelling, topping up with engine oil and checking the tyres. It was hot during the day under the clear skies, but as night fell it became refreshingly cool. The car ran beautifully for some 17 hours, breaking many records from 122.66 to 127.00 mph. At just over 17 hours, the engine blew, when John Gordon Benett was at the wheel.

The weather was beginning to break up, with rising winds and a forecast of rain. We packed it in, claiming that weather conditions had halted the runs. We could have fitted the spare engine and tried again for the 24-hour record, but we had decided to devote the next two days to long distance runs with the stock car. This ran with absolute reliability for 30 hours. By then, we felt we had collected all the records that mattered, including 24 hours at 104.30 mph and 5,000 kilometres at 103.93 mph.

It was now time for the publicity people to get to work and make the best use of the material provided by the team's efforts. During testing and during the actual record runs, a camera team had been shooting many feet of 16 mm cine film and this was made up into a publicity film with sound. Today, it is often shown to enthusiastic audiences at club meetings. For a comparatively small expenditure, real solid publicity for the new Austin Healey had been gained. The effects of this would last a long time and it had cost less than a few full page advertisements in national newspapers.

We hosed the cars down thoroughly with water, paying special attention to the underside, and then sprayed them with a dewatering oil that would lift the water off the metal surface and provide protection against salt corrosion. At least, that was the theory: in practice, it only retarded the inevitable attack of the rust bug, as salt had penetrated deeply into regions from where it could not be removed.

The team gathered up all the material for shipping back to England before walking the half-mile across the border of the dry state of Utah to the State Line Hotel in Nevada, to hold a celebration dinner. As always the conversation was of motor cars, the older members recalling previous record attempts at the salt flats.

We returned to England to pick up the next stage in the development of the Austin Healey.

The Cars of 1954

On our cars for 1954, we decided that we would use the then revolutionary disc brake system invented and developed by Dunlop in close co-operation with Jaguar. With the aid of these new brakes, the Jaguar XK120C and D types were to dominate the international sports car racing field for most of the 1950s and early 1960s. At that time, the disc brake system was handled by an offshoot of the Dunlop Aviation Division in Coventry and DMH was able to arrange with Joe Wright of Dunlop that they would provide us with the units we needed. We had always worked very closely with Dunlop, using their steel and wire wheels and their tyres. This was because Dunlop wheels and tyres were easily the best available, while the company's knowledge of high speed and racing tyres exceeded that of any other tyre manufacturer.

A Special Test car was built up based on the original specification with modifications to suit the disc brake installation. The system as devised by Dunlop consisted of large diameter half-inch thick steel discs with a hard chrome plate surface. The calipers were in effect four-piston versions of the six-piston brakes used by Jaguar. A steel caliper was mounted on the stub or swivel axle carrying an aluminium alloy twin cylinder assembly on each side of the disc. Each piston forced a circular pad of Mintex 875 material into contact with the disc under the influence of hydraulic pressure. Each piston and pad was fitted with positive retraction which drew the pads back to provide clearance between them and the disc in the off position. The hydraulic system was complicated. A Plessey hydraulic pump driven from

San Francisco, 1954.

the rear of the gearbox fed hydraulic fluid to one section of a very special tandem master cylinder. The pump system used a non-return valve, large bore high pressure hoses and a large reservoir. The handbrake mechanism, consisting of two levers carrying small pieces of friction material, was operated by cable from the handbrake lever.

In operation, pressure on the brake pedal applied pressure through a split system to the front and the rear brakes with additional power provided by the pump. In the event of hydraulic failure, only one axle set closed to provide stopping power.

Dunlop provided a set of parts for an installation check, including an aluminium disc. As usual the thickoes spotted this and it certainly caused their poorly developed little minds to boggle. We had arranged to use David Brown four-speed syncromesh gearboxes on the '54 series cars and

Austin designed the mounting and drive for the Plessey pump. Dunlop provided their centre lock peg drive aluminium alloy disc wheels of 16-inch diameter. Again, these wheels were similar to those used on the Jaguar competition vehicles, being very light and exceedingly strong. The rolled aluminium alloy rim and centre portion were pressed from a machined blank of the same alloy. We drew up and machined all the special hubs and parts.

It was not long before we had the Special Test vehicle built with one of the 1953 100 bhp engines. The brake performance was phenomenal, requiring only slight pedal pressure for maximum retardation with absolutely no sign of fade. In comparison with the best drum brakes we had tried, the new disc brakes were sensational in their consistent stopping power. DMH and I consider that these were the most powerful brakes ever produced. One could lock all four wheels with low pedal effort at any speed as often as desired. 'Mort' Morris Goodall joined us as competition manager and carried out the track proving at Silverstone. Once the braking system had been approved, the construction of four cars for the 1954 season commenced.

Other features of the cars were:
    larger DAS 10 rear dampers
    stronger front anti-roll bars
    David Brown four-speed gearboxes
    Marston bag type fuel tanks
    Marston light alloy radiators
    engines with four port heads
    engine oil coolers
    Lucas electrics
    600 × 16 Dunlop racing tyres
    Borg and Beck clutches

Three of the cars, SPL 256 BN–258 BN, would be competition vehicles, while the fourth, SPL 259 BN, would have its bodywork modified to become the high speed record breaker or sprint car for the 1954 record attempts.

The first outing was planned for the Sebring 12-hour endurance race for sports cars in March, with Lance Macklin and George Huntoon as drivers. Mort Goodall went as team manager with Jock Reid, who was Roger's understudy and did much of the disc brake work, as mechanic. Organized by the Automobile Racing Club of Florida and run by Alec Ulmann and Reggie Smith, Sebring was one of the great classic motor races, with a tricky and sometimes dangerous circuit laid out on the disused airfield near Sebring town in mid-Florida. The hot Florida sunshine and abrasive surface gave rise to very rapid tyre wear. With its Dunlop disc brake equipment giving it the advantage of being able to go deeper into corners without

Sebring 1954. A variety of methods for marking out the circuit were used over the years.

braking, and its Austin four-cylinder engines providing good low speed torque, the car was a potential winner. In the race it ran very well until near the end when a rocker arm broke, when it was lying second to Stirling Moss in an Osca. Jock Reid was not able to effect a repair and settled for removing the broken pieces, leaving the car to run on three cylinders for the rest of the race. This jeopardized any chance of a win, and in fact we finished in third place, after Lance was overtaken by a Lancia driven by Rubirosa. If the failure had occurred on either of the outside rocker arms and if the tappet or cam follower had not jumped out, Jock could have repaired the engine in time for the car to hold second place. If Harry Weslake had discovered the weakness in the valve gear earlier, we could probably have cured the problem before the start.

Sebring 1954. Lance Macklin with the 100 S prototype.

The prototype 100 S at Sebring, 1954.

Harry Weslake had broken a rocker arm during test bed work a few days before the start of the race and had highlighted a potential source of trouble. An inquest and investigation into the failure revealed that a build up of tolerances in the valve gear could result in the valve springs becoming very close to coil bound, imposing very high loads on the rocker arms. When rebuilding any of the big four cylinder engines, it is a wise precaution to check that the valve springs are not coil bound or close to coil bound in full valve open position.

We had reservations about the handling of the cars on 16-inch diameter wheels with the added unsprung weight of the large disc brakes. It was not possible to fit 15-inch wheels to the cars and carry out a back to back test to confirm this, but we decided that we would revert to 15-inch wheels for the next year's competition cars. For the remainder of the 1954 season, we decided to stick with the equipment as used at Sebring.

The work load on the experimental shop and design staff was very high. In addition to preparing the three Special Test cars for competition, we had to build the high speed car, refurbish the endurance car, build two fixed head coupés, develop and assess the Dunlop and Girling disc brake systems using 15-inch wheels, update and make improvements to the production 100, and investigate the many ideas devised by DMH, including a limited production competition car, the 100 S. We were also considering the change from four to six cylinder engines.

The next outing for the Special Test cars was the Mille Miglia in April, when they were driven by Lance Macklin, Tommy Wisdom and Mort Goodall, and Louis Chiron. The Mille Miglia was run over 1,000 miles of Italian roads in April or May, a time when the rainy season was often in full swing. We had already submitted homologation papers for an Austin Healey 100 S as a sports car, including all possible options. We entered the three cars in the Gran Turismo category where we had a very good chance of an outright win, but the Italian organizers said, in that very pleasant way of theirs, 'Yes, they could be GT but in our view a car capable of beating a Lancia sports at Sebring must be a sports car.' So the cars had to run in the over 2,000 cc sports category against an entry of eighteen Ferraris, two Maseratis, four Aston Martins and ten of the new and very fast Lancias.

At 9 on Saturday night the first of the slower small cars started from the raised platform built on the outskirts of Brescia on the road to Lake Garda and Verona. As the race was organized by the Automobile Club of Brescia,

Tommy Wisdom and Mort Goodall on the Mille Miglia starting ramp with the 100 S prototype.

the start was always well attended by local enthusiasts who stayed up all night until the big boys left in the early hours of the morning. The numbers on the cars signified the starting times for each entry and we were in the 05.00 hours group. Lance started with the first of our cars at 5.50 on Sunday morning. He would have to attend to all his own refuelling except at two points at which Roger would be on hand – Ravenna and then Bologna, which Roger would reach cross-country after refuelling and checking the oil on all three cars. Chiron had a leak from the rear brakes and retired between Ravenna and Pescara. Tommy Wisdom was seven minutes slower than Lance to Pescara; after Rome he started losing power until finally a valve dropped and went through a piston. He kept going for another 200 miles when one of the bits went through the sump and he lost oil pressure. He and Mort managed to get a tow to Bologna, from where Roger towed them back to Brescia. Lance made the finish looking as spruce as ever, with the car in good heart. He was 23rd out of 179 finishers, fifth in class, and the second foreign and first British driver. Alberto Ascari won the race in a Lancia 3.3 litre sports car at an average speed of 87 mph, whereas Lance had averaged 74 mph. The last car to finish in the class took no less than 23 hours 44 minutes!

Chiron's car had lost a brake bleed screw from the rear caliper, despite the fact that these were locked with wire. We quickly fixed this and set off for the Gotthard Pass, with Tommy's car on a tow rope. I drove Chiron's car with the aim of trying to find out what caused the failure. Sure enough, in the first 100 miles the brakes failed at well over 100 mph. I was able to bring the car to rest easily enough on the remaining front brakes, although without the advantage of power assistance the rate of deceleration was very unsatisfactory. We then spotted that a manufacturing fault in the handbrake mechanism had allowed one of the hand brake clappers to touch the bleed screw and loosen it. So we had learnt something.

Dunlop were now well advanced with a smaller, simpler and less expensive disc brake system which used a single piston on either side of the disc and did not require a pump. As on the more complex system, the brake calipers and hydraulics still had to be dismantled before the pads could be replaced. However, from data generated from racing, it was calculated that these brakes would last any of the long-distance races without a pad change.

The work on the Special test cars now consisted of converting them to the new brakes and 15-inch wire wheels. Meanwhile, DMH and Gerry Coker were busy with styling changes that were to produce the production 100 S.

The third of the original Special Test cars, NOJ 392, was loaned to Girling to be fitted with their new disc brakes. Girling, whose knowledge of vehicle braking systems was greater than that of any company outside of the USA, had developed a brake incorporating features that were widely

The first production 100 S, showing unused disc brakes.

copied in later years by the majority of brake manufacturers. In place of circular pads, Girling had devised large segmental pads which could be changed without dismantling the hydraulic system. The piston seals were cunningly designed so that they pulled the piston back a controlled amount following brake application, thus avoiding the need for complex mechanical retraction of the pads. In theory there were shortcomings in the Girling design, such as tapered pad wear and loss of stopping power in wet conditions, but in practice they worked very well. We tested them over many thousands of miles on road and track while Austin also subjected them to searching tests. Apart from a slight reduction in efficiency in wet conditions, neither of us could find any fault in their operation.

For the 100 S, however, we felt morally committed to use Dunlop brakes, as Dunlop had done all the spade work and kept us in the forefront of their progress before Girling were in a position to assist us. At the same time, we fitted Dunlop disc brakes to a production 100 and to the first of the 100 fixed head coupés, ONX 113, so that we could obtain more data on their performance under normal use.

The two special projects occupying our activities to the fullest were the two cars for the 1954 record runs. The 1953 endurance car was re-equipped with another variant of Dunlop disc brakes, a small lightweight unit that would cope with the infrequent application required during record breaking. These brakes were fitted with the Dunlop 16-inch peg drive light alloy wheels. By using the low ratio axles developed for the 100 S, we were able to dispense with the overdrive, eliminating the slight power loss caused by this form of transmission. At Austin, Don Hawley and John Barnett were hard at work extracting more power for us, by improving the 100 S power unit. The output was raised from 132 at 4,700 rpm to 142 at 4,600 rpm and new connecting rods were produced to avoid any chance of the sort of failure we had in 1953. The car was completely rebuilt with meticulous care.

Meanwhile, Gerry Coker had been working on body modifications for the sprint car, SPL 259 BN. It had been decided that a really high speed would have great publicity value, and no less than 200 mph was the allotted target figure. Most record attempts are made using a vehicle designed from scratch as a single-seater and using very little in the way of standard components. The MG record breakers, perhaps the most famous of all, were very special, following on from Reid Railton's original design for the car in which Major Goldie Gardner did over 148 mph in 1937.

In contrast, the Healey for 1954 was based on a standard chassis and body, albeit a light alloy unit, with the nose and tail extended from the wheel centres. This, of course, fixed the frontal area at a fairly high figure for a high speed machine. Gerry produced a quarter-sized clay model which was tested and assessed by Armstrong Whitworth Aircraft in their high speed wind tunnel at Coventry. They had tremendous experience of model testing and relating results to full size machines, but, like most wind tunnel specialists, they had reservations about the effects of testing a stationary model on a fixed platform. The difficulty was to calculate the effect of a moving vehicle running on solid ground. The figures used for the rolling

Gerry Coker and Roger Menadue take a critical look at the product.

The 100 S engined streamliner, the most beautiful of the record breaking cars, at speed in 1954.

resistance of tyres at high speed were also somewhat speculative. Very accurate predictions were possible for tyres operating up to 120 mph, but beyond that speed the figures then available were of doubtful accuracy. Armstrong Whitworth indicated that we would need 240 bhp at sea level to achieve 200 mph. They made a number of suggestions as to where we could make changes to improve wind resistance and thus increase speed. The main benefits were to be gained from positioning the air intake low down and keeping it as small as possible. Forcing air through a radiator at high speed takes a lot of power and produces high drag. In the rarefied world of John Cobb, Reid Railton had eliminated this problem by cooling the engine with large tanks of ice and water.

George Eyston wanted a fin as an aid to directional stability, and Gerry duly styled a beautiful appendage to the tail. The aerodynamic experts were inclined to pooh-pooh the concept of a fin and in fact we never had the occasion to prove or disprove its effectiveness at 200 mph, although current opinion tends to be favourable. It did have one undeniable advantage in that it extended the height of the car and made it visible at a greater distance.

The modifications to the body were carried out by Lionel Rawson at Slough who had already produced a number of all-metal bodies for Healey and Jowett chassis, including the Sportsmobile. With Gerry's drawings and assistance from Roger, Lionel fabricated the two ends and welded these to the body. Inside these extensions were light alloy diaphragms or bulkheads, flush riveted in position. The actual construction of the body was completed in six weeks. Gerry took charge of the painting, adding the distinctive lightning flash to the fin, the side flash and a stripe on the bonnet in blood red, contrasting with the Healey ice blue paintwork. The total effect was very exciting.

Austin were preparing the power unit in the East Works at Longbridge. The research department there, under the charge of Doc John Weaving, included a wind tunnel which would accept full size motor cars. The preparation of the unit was left to Bill Leland, an engine man of the old school. To get the required power it was necessary to supercharge or blow the engine, and we decided to use one of the superchargers manufactured by Noel and Chris Shorrock. These were produced by the two brothers in very small quantities, and were available in a variety of sizes. They recommended a unit that would give us the desired degree of boost and which had been proved to be very efficient and reliable. It was driven directly from the front of the crankshaft, coupled on via a short shaft with two Layrub couplings. A large SU carburettor with two float chambers fed the fuel/air mixture to the blower. The inlet manifolds were fabricated in steel with rubber hose joints. The fuel tank was located in the tail of the car, fuel being drawn off by four SU large capacity single electric fuel pumps and delivered via a half-inch pipe to the carburettor.

The engine was modified with low compression pistons and a cast iron 100 S-type cylinder head. To cope with the high cylinder pressures, the water transfer passages in the head and block face were plugged, the coolant being piped from the rear of the block to the rear of the head. This ensured that any gas leakage at the joint face would not get into the coolant and that coolant could not be lost at this point.

Bill Leland did not have long to build and tune the engine and was hampered by a fuel distribution problem, which he finally solved by using wire gauze in the manifold. The fuel used was a mixture of 66.2:3 per cent Methanol and 33.1:3 per cent Benzole, with 11 cc of castor oil added to each gallon of mixture. The boost pressure was 9.6 lb per square inch. Once Bill had obtained a reliable 224 bhp at 4,500 rpm, with the engine running flat out, Roger completed the engine installation and Doc Weaving put the car into Austin's wind tunnel. He carried out a series of tests and calculated the results, predicting that it would achieve 192 mph, with a possible 2–3 mph increase if conditions were ideal. In retrospect, we should have opted for a higher boost pressure, lower compression ratio and a surplus of power over the estimated figure required, but time was very short.

We bought a five-speed gearbox from David Brown, one of a small number made for a large-engined Lagonda. This was amply strong and had a fifth gear overdrive ratio. Borg and Beck provided a suitable clutch. We used the original BN1 100 S type rear axle with spiral bevel gearing. The advantage of this was that it was a simple matter to design a ratio of 2.47 to 1. To produce a given ratio with a hypoid bevel gear set, as used in the BN2 series, requires many calculations and special tooling.

Roger Menadue putting the bubble canopy on the streamliner with DMH at the wheel.

Despite the widely circulated view that car manufacturers were not interested in safety, we were always very conscious of the need to make safe vehicles. In the case of the sprint car, we were aware that we had a fuel pumping system that could deliver over 500 pints of fuel and thus prove very dangerous for the driver. To make this safe we fitted the engine with a pressure switch in the oil system that would cut the electric pumps instantly in the event of an engine blow up. An over-ride spring-loaded push button enabled the pumps to be set into action when the engine was started up. In addition, Graviner – the experts in aircraft and armoured vehicle fire-fighting equipment – provided a pressurized extinguisher system that would flood the engine and fuel compartments with chloro bromo methane to kill any fire. The system could be operated manually by the driver, by pressing a fire button in the centre of the wheel, and automatically by switches sensitive to impact or vehicle inversion. Similar, more advanced systems are fitted to today's Formula One racing cars and have been very valuable in increasing driver safety.

Dunlop provided tyres with strong casings and very thin rubber treads to stand up to the forces involved at 200 mph. The braking system was identical to that used on the endurance car.

We did some shakedown runs at Gaydon. The engine was started by switching on, pressing the fuel over-ride button and then the starting button. With 'soft' plugs fitted – that is, plugs that would not oil up easily – it would be run up with small throttle openings and moderate rpm until it was nicely warm. On start up there would be a few coughs and bangs until the engine caught, whereupon it would settle down to a thundering 1,000 rpm while a cloud of smoke cleared away from the exhaust. It was then stopped to allow the 'hard' plugs, that would stand full power, to be fitted. I did several runs up the main runway, gradually building up speed. I tried all the gears, finding the gear change heavy and ponderous, and reached just short of 160 mph before I had to apply the brakes. One hears much about the sensation of speed but in actual fact this was negligible until one saw the braking-point marker and the rapidly approaching end of the runway surface. One was, of course, continuously aware of the position of the tachometer needle as it climbed round the dial. The cockpit had been constructed to suit DMH and I found it rather cramped. The near solidly mounted four cylinder caused a fair amount of vibration but what I remember is the continuous surge of acceleration and the very high directional stability of the machine. The stability and ease of control were a direct result of the very effective shape of the vehicle, which showed none of the dreaded front-end lift so noticeable with many high speed machines. Apart from a rectangular wheel, the steering and suspension were all standard, taken from the production line.

The 1954 streamliner prior to a demonstration run.

With the exception of the new 100 S, described in a separate chapter, these two record cars completed our programme of specials for 1954. On 31st July, the two cars and spares were loaded onto Austin trucks for transport to Southampton. And on 4th August, we set sail for New York aboard Cunard's *Mauretania*, to test the results of all our preparations to the limit once more, on the salt flats of Utah.

200 mph

We arrived in the USA with high hopes of achieving something sensational in the way of performance, armed with a pretty comprehensive set of data and information.

Once again, Fred Horner guided us through a hot and sticky New York. The change in climate at Bonneville was most welcome, being hot by day but relatively cool at night. The Austin men had unpacked the car and spare parts and Roger and I spent some time checking for shipping damage. Mercifully, this was very small and took but a short time to rectify.

At that time of year, the salt was in good condition. The straightaway had been scraped and swept, and the Utah State highway officials were in the process of laying the oil stripe down the centre. This black line, 9 inches wide, contrasted well against the dazzling white of the salt and would be the only feature that DMH would have by which to steer the car.

Before dawn the team were up and breakfasting at the motel restaurant, where the main problem was to persuade the staff to get the coffee machine to produce boiling water for our tea. We had the car loaded on a trailer and towed it out to the south end of the straightaway. We fitted the sprint wheels and tyres, fuelled it and then warmed it up on soft plugs. I ran it around gently to warm up the transmission and rear axle. When it had reached the right temperature, we fitted the hard spark plugs. DMH then climbed in and we clamped down the canopy. With dawn just breaking and with only a slight breeze, he set off on the run to the north end of the straightaway. Accelerating gently from rest over the rough salt surface, he

The 1954 streamliner fitted with the aeroscreen for 1-hour records.

built up speed once he reached the scraped surface. On the vast salt lake the car was but an insignificant dot as it disappeared over the horizon. We jumped into the support vehicles and hurried up one side of the course. Salt conditions were poor at this end, with soft patches, and we had difficulty in jacking the car up for Dunlop's tyre expert, Lysle Hysert, to check for cuts or damage from the run. DMH reported all the gauge readings and commented on how stable the car had felt. It all seemed to be right and so we sent him off on the return run. Part-way down the timed section, the engine hiccoughed and went off song. DMH switched off and coasted to the end of the straightaway where he waited for us to catch up. We whipped out the spark plugs for examination. Under expert examination, these can give a very good indication of what is happening or has happened in an engine. Number two plug was obviously not firing, being black and oily. We fitted a new set but this failed to make the engine fire on four cylinders and a compression check revealed that number two cylinder was badly down. We then decided to abandon the runs until after we had put matters right. The car had broken the 5 kilometre record at 179.63 mph, which was some consolation.

Back at base we set to, to remove the cylinder head – a difficult job, as it was stuck. Jimmy Harrison, who should have known better, stood astride the top of the bonnet and attempted to lift it out, succeeding only in denting the bodywork where his plimsoled feet took the strain. Eventually we managed to lift it clear and were rewarded by a sorry sight: the top of one piston was burnt and the aluminium had coated the valves with aluminium beads. Syd Enever and Alec Hounslow were on hand with the MG record car and offered us their help and advice, which we gladly accepted. Syd Enever was one of those experienced and highly competent engineers, so sadly missing in today's automobile industry.

A plan of action was drawn up to enable us to run the car the next morning. All the pistons and rods were removed and the cylinder head studs extracted. The cylinder bores were honed to remove all score marks and provide a little more piston clearance. The most laborious and time-consuming job was to lap the cylinder head to the block. After coating the head face with coarse carborundum valve grinding compound, two men, one at either end, had to push it backwards and forwards across the top surface of the cylinder block. We took this task in turns until we had produced a perfect mating fit between the head and block faces. All traces of grinding compound were then carefully removed and the pistons and rods refitted. Reeves Dutton, the AAA's technical official, measured the bores to check that we had kept the engine within class limits. A great deal of work with the hones had increased their size by only two-thousandths of an inch. The joint faces were then coated with Seccotine glue and the head carefully torqued down to specified figures. After it had been assembled with fresh oil, the engine functioned normally.

The crew: Lysle Hysert, Roger Menadue, Reeves Dutton, an unknown, Jack Ryan, Ken Harris, an unknown, Jimmy Harrison, Ralph Le Hew, George Perry, George Eyston, four unknowns, and the author.

Bonneville salt flats, 1954. DMH at the wheel of the 100 S before the start of the 24-hour record run. In the background: Mort Goodall, Carroll Shelby, George Eyston and Roy Jackson-Moore. Lysle Hysert of Dunlop is looking at the special tyres.

We decided that the probable cause of the failure was a weak mixture – the normal culprit in such cases. If in doubt, it is safe to richen up the mixture and fit a grade colder spark plug. We first checked the output of the fuel pumps against a stop watch, but these proved to have more than double the required output. Jimmy Harrison then stripped the carburettor and rebuilt it with a higher fuel level setting and a considerably richer needle. When using an alcohol-based fuel, it is possible to richen the mixture well beyond that required for maximum power, resulting in a very small power loss but considerably improved internal cooling.

Early on 22nd August, we left base for the salt flats so that when dawn broke we had the car warmed up and ready for DMH. That morning's runs down the straightaway were completed without any mechanical trouble, with a two-way average for the kilometre of 192.74 mph. In addition, the car broke the international class records for 5 km, 5 miles, 10 km and 10 miles, at speeds from 182.26 to 181.08 mph. The engine was running as well at the end as it had been at the start.

Taking advantage of the timing system set up for the sprint car, DMH then tried the endurance car against the clock, reaching an average of

The 1954 24-hour record breaking 100 S with some of the crew. DMH, Jimmy Harrison of SU, George Perry of Lucas, an unknown, Ralph Le Hew of Champion, Roger Menadue shirtless, an unknown, and Jack Ryan of Austin.

142.22 mph over the kilometre. With the really high speed work completed, we were now set up for the endurance runs the following day.

We had established a time schedule for the 24 hours, which enabled the drivers taking over later to have a long lie-in. Not so the workers, who travelled to the flats after a hearty breakfast in the restaurant and had everything ready for the start at 7.48 am, with the car warmed up, full of fuel and oil, and with the tyres fitted. DMH took the start and the first three hours, followed by George Eyston, Carroll Shelby, Mort Goodall and Roy Jackson Moore, each taking three-hour stints. This time the car ran for 24 hours without incident, collecting a bag of long-distance records from 200 km to 5,000 km and 1 to 24 hours, at speeds of over 132 mph.

The next plan was to run the sprint car on the 10-mile circle for one hour, with racing driver Carroll Shelby at the wheel. For this distance we had to use the long-distance tyres with thicker treads and a maximum safe recommended speed of 160 mph. In order to fit Carroll Shelby's lanky frame into the car, we replaced the perspex canopy with one of our small aero screens. This run started just before 10 am, after we had finished the 24-hour run. Carroll Shelby drove to our instructions, keeping the car circulating at just under the 160 mph limit, and breaking all the records for 25 to 200 kilometres plus the one hour mark, at 157.92 mph.

In all, the 1954 runs gave us a large number of worthwhile records, setting a high of 192.74 mph. Our arch rivals in the American sports car market, Triumph, were unable to produce anything approaching our performance.

We were all delighted, but DMH was still determined to better 200 mph in an Austin Healey.

The next opportunity to demonstrate the high speed reliability of the Austin Healey came with the arrival of the Morris-designed six cylinder of 2,639 cc capacity. On paper, this more modern engine, with its large valves and ports and shorter stroke, seemed far superior to Austin's rugged old four banger. Originally conceived as a passenger car engine to replace the lusty four in BMC's model range, the six was in fact to set us many problems. A record breaking expedition was included in the competition programme for 1956 to give a publicity boost to the engine before it was released to the public. Our aim was to exceed 200 mph and raise the distance records up to six hours.

For the six-hour car, we took the 1953/4 endurance car, SPL 227/B, and extended the nose and tail sections beyond the wheel centres. The wheel base remained unchanged from the original four-cylinder figure of 90 inches. Gerry Coker took great care to produce a streamlined form of pleasing appearance. He paid careful attention to detail, including the design of a grille over the air intake which used horizontal bars of wavy form. This he would later expand and fine up as the 100 Six grille. The body modifications were carried out by Jensen to his instructions. They moaned about the difficulty of welding the new ends to the old panels of the body, but although there were some problems due to salt corrosion, I suspect their griping was really a ploy to extract more money for the job. This car was completed using the existing 100 S type rear axle and gearbox, and a highly tuned six-cylinder engine.

Eddie Maher and Jack Goffin at Morris Engines undertook to build the engines at Coventry, and were also responsible for supplying Austin with the special engine parts for the supercharged engine. Many components of the engines were special – the rods, crankshafts, pistons, camshafts, cylinder heads, valves and valve gear. The heads of six port form had six separate inlet ports – the first stage in a development that was to end with the last 3000.

Bill Leland was again responsible for the construction and development of the supercharged engine under the control of Doc Weaving. To provide the designed boost pressure, a Rootes-type supercharger made by Marshall was driven by a chain from the front of the engine. The chain drive enabled the blower drive ratio to be fixed to give the desired amount of boost. This chain drive was later to give trouble. Bill Leland had a lot of problems initially with minor engine blow-ups on the test bed and delays in getting the special parts. In the end, the engine was developed to the state where it gave 292 bhp, over three times the output of the basic engine in production form. Today, the American exhaust-driven turbo charger has replaced the

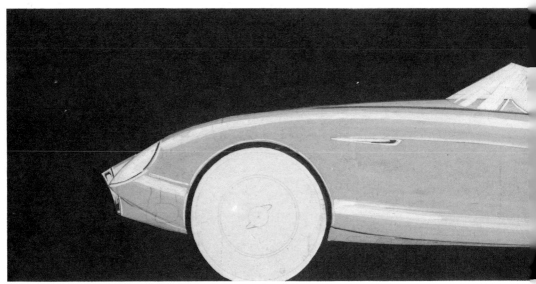

A styling drawing for the first six-cylinder competition cars, based on a standard centre section. The lamps were not enclosed on the cars as built: this was less dramatic but probably a benefit when racing at night.

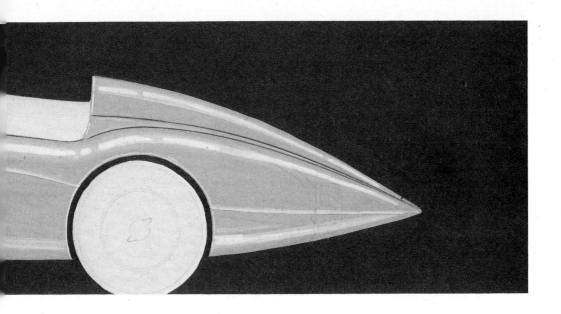

Dated 18th March 1954, this styling idea was produced by Gerry Coker for an Austin Healey grille which was later incorporated on the 3000.

mechanically driven supercharger, by virtue of its higher efficiency, and greater reliability and ease of installation.

The modifications to the sprint car body were extensive, involving a reduction in the frontal area to reduce the drag at speed. It is sad to reflect that these modifications left so little of the original car unchanged. In fact, it would have been less costly had we started with a completely new body, and in that case the old car could still be on view in some museum, enabling today's enthusiasts to appreciate its grace and beauty. Since much of the original running gear was replaced in the interests of safety, very little of the original was retained, apart from some of the panel work and the chassis frame. The calculated and tested power requirements for 200 mph did show that the modified body required less power than the original, but we have always felt that with the increased power of the six the old car would have exceeded 200 mph.

For a third time, we proceeded to Utah with most of the original crew. George Eyston, who had been ill, brought along George Williams, also of Castrol, to help with the organization. We unpacked and repaired the cars, which had suffered some slight damage on the long trip from Warwick. We had always been made very welcome by the local people and officials, and old acquaintances displayed great pleasure at our arrival.

This year we were confident that we would exceed 200 mph, after coming close in 1954. We thought little had been left to chance, for with some 70 more horsepower and reduced drag the car had a predicted top speed of 217 mph. Prior to our departure for the USA, Ron Flockhart had tested the car for us over several laps of the high-speed banked circuit at MIRA. There were no problems with these tests.

We mixed the fuel and got everything ready for a dawn test run. Dawn is usually the best time as the air is then at its lowest temperature and wind speeds are low. The wind tends to increase as the sun rises and the air warms up.

Early the next morning, 9th August, we assembled at the south end of the straightaway, fitted the high speed tyres, and warmed up the engine and transmission before changing the spark plugs to Champion NA12 racing plugs. DMH got in the cockpit and we clamped on the canopy. He then accelerated steadily up the straightaway, changing up through the gears. In fifth gear he had accelerated to over 200 mph when there was a loud explosion, and flames and smoke shot upwards from the exhaust stacks on top of the bonnet. When he had coasted to rest, we found that the blower drive had broken, which meant that the car had to be taken back to base for repair.

We then tried out the endurance car but this was not very inspiring. It tended to miss at speed and was not reaching the calculated speed. After the car had stopped it proved very difficult to restart, as the hot exhaust manifolds were heating the inlet manifolds and boiling the fuel in the carburettors. We removed the inlet manifolds and filed them to provide clearance from the exhaust manifolds, and then arranged a duct to blow cold air across. We also put additional lagging on the fuel lines in the engine compartment. A further run showed a definite improvement and the car was deemed to be satisfactory for the runs scheduled for 11th August. We did not have exclusive use of the salt flats and had to give way to others who had booked them.

Back at the base, we stripped the sprint car's blown engine for inspection. The blower drive was a mess, with a broken chain and a mangled crankshaft sprocket. The cylinder bores had slight scores and three pistons showed signs of having picked up. We filed and polished the piston skirts to increase the clearance and honed the cylinder bores to remove most of the scoring. No one present could find any apparent reason for the problem – and that included several experienced racing officials, George Eyston, DMH, Roger and myself, altogether a fair collection of men experienced in looking at blown engines. The engine was rebuilt with as much care as possible and seemed to be perfect when restarted.

On 14th August, Carroll Shelby set off round the 10-mile circle in the long-distance car. After six laps, it lost power and went rough. A check revealed that compression had been lost in one cylinder – obviously another rebuild job. The cylinder head was removed to reveal trouble in number one cylinder. One valve had a badly carboned stem and was not seating properly. The water ways in the block and the cylinder head did not line up correctly, failing to seal on the ferrules in the gasket. We checked the spare cylinder head and found the same error in the water passage positions. Using Roger's favourite compound for sealing gaskets, a mixture of Hermatite and aluminium paint, we refitted the head. We ran the rebuilt engine up to normal operating temperature and torqued the head down, and then checked the valve clearances. We decided that we would have to be very careful not to overstrain the engine and accordingly reduced the scheduled speeds for the record attempt.

Carroll Shelby again took the start at 05.55 on 16th August. We maintained a very close and somewhat nervous watch on the run, Carroll maintaining the speed we signalled to him on each lap. After 50 laps we called him in for refuelling and for Roy Jackson Moore to take over. Two hours later the engine started to overheat. Roy stopped at the pits and we refilled the cooling system with water and Wondarweld, a leak-stopping compound. From now on, the scheduled speed was lower and Roy carried on till the engine expired some 80 miles short of the 1,000-mile distance. The gasket had blown again but we had broken the records from 200 miles

The 100 Six and 6-hour record car at the 1956 Motor Show.

to 1,000 kilometres at speeds from 151.27 to 153.58 mph, and the six-hour record at 146.07 mph. Fuel consumption worked out at 12.52 mpg.

Our next booking for the straightaway was on Sunday, 19th August. On his first run north, DMH exceeded 200 mph according to the official timing, but on the return run the engine blew up again. We now had a real problem as we needed spares from England and our time on the flats was drawing to a close. At Wendover all overseas calls had to be made from the railway station where the telephone exchange, telegraph, ticketing and station buffet were all run by one efficient woman. She got on the line and soon located Doc Weaving in England. I explained all our problems and told him what I thought we needed. Less than 24 hours later, we had all the bits and rebuilt the engine again.

On 21st August we again went to the start. DMH was instructed to take it easy and reserve full power for the timed distance only. The north run went well, with an average speed of 203.76 mph. On the return run, the engine failed again in the timed distance and DMH had to coast. He was rewarded by a two-way average of 203.11 mph. Naturally, he was delighted that he had achieved his ambition and managed to exceed 200 mph.

We had now collected a very valuable bag of class records over the three years and it was decided that this was enough. Record breaking was in danger of losing its publicity value as we and MG had done it so often.

The two record cars lay at the Cape at Warwick for some years, with no further use envisaged for them. Carroll Shelby contacted us in the 1960s, when he was well involved with the Shelby Cobras, to see if we would let him have the 200 mph car for some record attempts with one of his Ford engines. Roger and I had a good look at the old car but decided that corrosion had done too much damage and that it could not be made into a safe high speed vehicle again. I do not think we were over cautious as we all had a great admiration for Carroll and his efforts in motor racing and made a very thorough investigation into all the possibilities.

Both cars were finally stripped of any useful equipment and cut up and sold as scrap.

The 100 S

Profit, that one good reason, had no part in the considerations that caused the 100 S to be produced. The car was built in limited numbers to fulfil a number of purposes. It was to be a competition vehicle that would gain exposure on the world's race tracks and help increase the Austin Healey's sporting image. It would provide a base vehicle that would form the starting point for the Austin Healey competition programme, to gain publicity for the marque. It would be a developed competition vehicle which could compete in international events without modification.

The 100 S was one of the most highly developed cars to reach production. Starting with the original 100, it was developed through the 1953 and 1954 competition vehicles, incorporating many small improvements found necessary for racing purposes.

The assembly of the production frame was redrawn to incorporate small strengthening gussets round the lower wishbone attachment points. Strengthening gussets were also added to the steering gear and idler mounting brackets, and stronger brackets were fitted at the rear to carry the larger DAS 10 shock absorbers. Sundry other small gussets were added with the aim of increasing the strength of the frame. In themselves these parts cost little, but assembly was costly. These reinforcements had been developed on the Special Test cars and were always added to the later six-cylinder competition cars. Complete details of these modifications were passed to Marcus Chambers for incorporation on the successful rally cars that the BMC competitions department constructed at Abingdon.

A 100 S as new, photographed in the park at Warwick.

Part of the six 100 S cars being loaded at Warwick for the 1955 Sebring race. Briggs Cunningham's car, with his special paint combination, is upper left.

John Thompson produced these frames completely modified and delivered them to Jensen Motors at West Bromwich. On this base Jensen built the bodies, using many light alloy parts in the understructure. Aluminium alloy panels were pressed on the production tools and hand finished by Jensen's excellent team of sheet metal workers – tin bashers, as they were commonly called. The tinsmiths union was very strong and protected the jobs of its workers. Entry to the union was by way of a craft apprenticeship, which in turn was dependent upon being a close relative of an existing member. The tinsmiths worked on all sheet metal up to 14 SWG (Imperial Standard Wire Gauge) or 0.080 inches thickness. Any sheet metal in excess of these dimensions was the province of the boiler makers. Dick Jensen used to become very frustrated when union policy forced him to use these highly skilled and expensive men on simple operations that could be done by unskilled men. One hazard of sheetmetal work, because of the noise generated by continuous hammering and beating, was early loss of hearing.

Externally the styling changes that gave the car its distinctive appearance were the work of DMH and Gerry Coker, plus a few ideas from my brother Brian, who was something of an artist. Many of the body features of the Special Test cars were refined and improved for this production. From the front, the major visual difference was the smaller grille, which had softer lines than that on the 100. DMH and Gerry worked this out on one of the

A 100 S being photographed outside the works at the Cape. The back view was particularly pleasing when uncluttered by a bumper.

The 100 S

Special Test cars. The body shell had a few small modifications and was skinned entirely in aluminium, to save weight. The rear wings had a crease line that ran from the front wheel arch back along the side of the body to the front of the rear wheel and was extended through to the rear of the car. This was developed by Gerry and was easy to add to the cars in small numbers.

This crease line provided a break point for the two-tone paintwork. Like other leaders of the industry, DMH paid a great deal of attention to colour selection, although we never felt the need for the vast army of colour consultants, interior designers and other self-opinionated experts employed by many of the big companies. He spent many hours studying painted samples with Gerry and quite a number of cars were painted in various colour schemes. Only a complete car can give the full visual impact of a particular colour: it is impossible to make a valid assessment from a single panel alone. DMH finally decided that the bodywork above the crease line should be white, while the lower sides were painted in lobelia, a rich blue produced by Dockers.

Even so, a body finished in aluminium is a beautiful piece of art, and it is a shame that it has to be covered in paint! Jensen painted and trimmed the bodies, made and fitted the perspex windscreen, and built and trimmed the special seats. These were drawn up by Gerry and incorporated three trimmed slots in the back rest, designed to keep the driver's back comfortably cool.

Brian Healey in the first production 100 S, outside the experimental shop at the Cape.

*The 100 S power unit
in the experimental shop
on its transport cradle.*

The 100 S could not have been made without the whole-hearted support of Austin. George Harriman agreed the concept of the vehicle with DMH and the use of the Austin Healey name. Austin undertook to supply the special components required while responsibility for the supply of power units was passed on to Morris Motors. Jimmy Thompson, their chief engineer, Jack Low and Eddie Maher drew up the modifications and the engines were produced in limited numbers at the Morris engine plant at Courthouse Green, Coventry, alongside the production 100 engines.

In the original design, Harry Weslake had drawn the manifold joint face at an angle to the vertical. This facilitated the casting of inlet manifolds but made the construction of the exhaust manifold difficult, as it required a very acute bend from the joint face to the downward facing pipes. Morris Engines altered this assembly to obtain a vertical angle, and made a number of other small detail changes. The specified output of 132 bhp at 4,700 rpm was obtained on all production engines.

The valve seats were based on a Nash Motors recommendation, being fitted with a taper on the outer diameter designed to prevent them coming out. This made replacement a more difficult operation. With this valve seat arrangement there was a very thin section of aluminium between the inlet and exhaust seats which could cause problems. Morris Engines later overcame this when they produced the aluminium heads for the competition six-cylinder engines, by using seats cast in pairs like a figure of eight or spectacles. The old Austin-designed valve cotters or keepers with their sharp necking of the valve stem were replaced by valves having two annular grooves of semi-circular cross section at the top, which were fitted with very accurately ground cotters of matching form. These cotters, variously known as bullock, bulldog or dual groove, permitted the minimum diameter of the stem to be increased and reduced the stress concentration at this point. These cotters were produced in matched pairs and it is important that anyone rebuilding an engine should keep each pair of cotters with its own valve. The valve springs and seats were redesigned to reduce stresses and to avoid any chance of the valve springs becoming solid or coil bound when the valves were fully open.

The 100 S cylinder block was different from that of the 100 with the studs located in a configuration which allowed better disposition of the valve porting. The top deck of the block had the internal thickening or bossing altered to suit this stud arrangement. Particular attention was paid to the machining of the crankshaft sealing face in which the oil retaining scroll functioned. Austin engines tended to lose oil in this area when operated at higher engine speeds.

The crankshaft was similar to the 100, except that it was forged in EN40B, machined and nitride hardened. The bearing journals were then polished. The treated steel shaft had tensile strength in the range of 60 to 70 tons per square inch. The shaft and flywheel were accurately balanced, the flywheel being machined out of a billet of high carbon steel to resist scoring of the clutch face. This flywheel was considerably lighter than the cast iron one used in the production 100 engine. The nitride hardened crankshaft was carried in tri-metal bearings of indium lead bronze with thin steel shells, manufactured by Vandervell. These were the best bearings available.

The sump or oil pan was increased in capacity to 20 imperial pints by means of a sheet steel extension to the forward end of the oil pan.

The pistons were of the solid skirt type, having no slots in this area. The piston ring pack consisted of two narrow compression rings with a one-piece oil control ring. The pistons had large clearances and would rattle in the bores when cold but would quickly quieten as they warmed and expanded.

The valve timing was mild, using the optional camshaft available for the 100. Valve clearance was always 0.015 inches set with the engine cold. Valve lift was 0.435 inches and the valve opening overlap only 25 degrees.

Lucas made a special version of their 22290 competition dynamo to suit the mounting position. We had some trouble with the first production engines due to the engines being tested before the dynamos had been connected to an electrical load. This was overcome by running the engines with the brushes lifted off the commutator.

The gearbox was a close ratio version of the 'C' series gearbox, with a side-mounted change lever. Overdrive was not used but was listed as an optional extra.

Morris Engines ran in each engine on the test bed, taking the power at the rear of the gearbox. After running in, a full throttle power test was made using a slave S exhaust system.

100 S cars raised on trestles so that the axles and front suspensions could be fitted.

100 S rear brake assembly, with the separate hand brake mechanism above the caliper.

A 100 S and the red and black coupé outside the experimental shop at the Cape.

The supply of engines was somewhat erratic and the first ones took a long time to arrive. They were usually sent warm from the test bed, with sticky paint. I was frequently calling up Eddie Maher and Jack Goffin to urge delivery. After the formation of BMC, Austin were very much the dominant partners, driving the Morris organization to distraction. Morris Engines, but a small off-shoot in Coventry, consequently got hammered from every quarter. Len Lord had some justification in trying to knock the giant into shape but unfortunately many of his junior subordinates proceeded to ape and even exceed his efforts. Morris Engines only survived by dint of good hard work.

The bodies were collected from Jensen and set up on two wooden trestles so that all the pipe work, suspension and axles could be fitted from underneath. The assembly was then lowered onto the shop floor for the installation of the engine, fuel tank and radiator, this lowering being achieved by means of two 15 cwt garage cranes. Following racing practice, many nuts and bolts were wire locked for security, which meant that the bolt heads had to be drilled with small electric hand drills. Brake bleeding, filling with oils and wheel alignment immediately preceded a road test. Roger or I tested every 100 S produced, over a run of about 20 miles. The most frequent rectification needed was to rebleed the brakes and cure the not acceptable oil leaks. S engines had a tendency to leak oil round the tubes in the cylinder head that enclosed the push rods.

The brakes were the latest single-pot spot type, with a wheel cylinder either side of the disc operating Mintex brake pads. The discs were machined from steel billets and were not plated. They were not really satisfactory as the flat braking surface tended to distort in conical form to as much as 30 thousandths of an inch, giving rise to excessive pedal travel.

The first cars to come off the Cape assembly line were destined for the USA, where they were to run in the 12 Hour Grand Prix of Endurance at Sebring in March 1955. They therefore had to be thoroughly tested whilst any damage to their paintwork had to be most strenuously avoided. Some trouble was experienced with gear selection due to a faulty shifter fork, which necessitated removing the gearboxes. This last-minute change caused the working of yet more overtime to enable us to meet the scheduled sailing for New York.

We had put considerable development time into arriving at a suitable gearbox, starting with the special wide-ratio taxi gearboxes. For the next generation of cars we had used David Brown four-speed gearboxes as used by Aston Martin. David Brown are amongst Europe's best gear manufacturers and these boxes were strong with good shift qualities. However, it was almost impossible to prevent oil loss through the front gearbox seal, which was not very nice for the clutch. The installation of the DB box in the

Healey required quite a few changes to the X member and rear mounting. Morris Engines lent us a close ratio 'C' series box for test which stood up to a full series of idiot starts without complaint and also had excellent sealing. The gear shifting was, if anything, superior to that of the DB box, and since this unit possessed the added advantage of being manufactured within the group, we had no hesitation in specifying it for the 100 S.

All the cars arrived safely in the USA and a total of seven took part in the first practice session. The factory car was driven by Stirling Moss and Lance Macklin, and proved to be quicker than most cars on the circuit. Stirling was probably the best driver around, the difficulty then – as today – being to build a car capable of standing up to the cornering forces and speeds that he could extract from it. Although he never exceeded any set engine speed, with him at the wheel, the car was always travelling as quickly as any man could drive it.

During practice an oil leak developed in the Superflexit oil hoses and the clutches were wearing badly. Cyril Fowler and the Austin workers obtained some American hose and fittings and fabricated some excellent replacements. The clutch problem was caused by some goon at Borg and Beck who had specified and fitted the wrong clamping springs. We found that the

A works 100 S – OON 440.

Jaguar assembly would fit and Ed Bussey of Ship and Shore scoured Florida for them. They arrived quickly, due to the excellence of the US transport system. Needless to say, the American owners were unhappy with the troubles with their new cars, but that soon changed once the new parts were fitted and they could get down to serious practice.

There was some concern in the camp as to how long the brake pads would last. Replacing the pads entailed a complete strip of the brakes followed by a lengthy bleeding process. Painstaking measurement of the pad thickness after practice, with some rapid wear calculation indicated that they could wear out in $11\frac{1}{2}$ hours. New pads were fitted and meticulously bedded in before the start: very careful bedding can prolong lining life.

Stirling and Lance went flat out from the start, well up in the midst of the Ferraris and Maseratis. The race was won by Mike Hawthorn and Phil Walters in a D Type Jaguar, followed by two Ferraris and two Maseratis, and with Stirling in sixth place. One 100 S fell by the wayside when one of the fabricated oil pipes failed but the other five all finished. Despite its lowly origin, that offended the purists, the 100 S was very competitive for 1955, matching the performance of the best sports racing cars then available, on any but the very fastest circuits. If anything, its good looks and high quality finish were not in keeping with the usual rough appearance of other sports racing cars.

Later that year, the works entered three cars in the Mille Miglia, while a fourth was entered by Charles Clark of Wolverhampton, to be driven by BRM driver Ron Flockhart. Ignoring the advice of the company's financial advisors, DMH decided to take part in the race with the Warwick

A works 100 S being prepared for the Mille Miglia. We used an aero screen as this could be adjusted to improve driver comfort.

The Austin Healey pits at Le Mans, with the Rover BRM car. Rover led the field in engineering with their gas turbine engines.

mechanic, Jim Cashmore, and had OON 439 equipped with a windscreen and hood. George Abecassis, in the red S, was the most successful, despite running out of petrol in the mountains short of Rome. He somehow managed to borrow some petrol from a spectator and made it to the next refuelling point. This delay cost him 52 places on the Aquila-Rome stage but he finally finished 11th overall with first place in class, and was the first British finisher.

Lance Macklin was the quickest of all on the first 303 kilometres but gradually dropped behind to finish in 36th position. Ron Flockhart lost his on a curve approaching a bridge, went through the parapet, and ended upside down in a stream some 30 feet below. He managed to extricate himself from the car and was carried to a nearby house, where he was stripped of all clothing and rubbed down with Italian brandy. When Margot and I arrived to collect him some hours later, he was completely recovered.

DMH and Jim Cashmore were forced to make frequent stops to add oil. They got around the course but were eliminated on the time taken. Although both enjoyed the day's drive, DMH was finally persuaded to give up racing and make better use of his talents. Stirling Moss won the race in a Mercedes in 10 hours 7 minutes, at an average of fractionally under 100 mph. This achievement naturally filled the front pages of the daily papers.

The next event was the ill-fated 24 Hours at Le Mans. Lance Macklin and Les Leston were entered in NOJ 393 and the engine preparation was left to Eddie Maher. The high-lift long-period camshaft was fitted, although it was originally designed for use with heavier sodium filled valves, as it gave the valve gear a much easier time despite a slight power increase, due to the lower acceleration rate. It lacked bottom-end torque but this would not be important at Le Mans. Carburation was via two 2-inch HD8 SUs. These larger SUs do undoubtedly give greater power on the S but they are finicky to tune. In this form the engine output was 140 bhp and the car would lap very quickly at over 100 mph.

Jaguar, who had won the race twice before, were running their beautiful D Types, fitted with the remarkable twin cam XK engine. The Jaguar engine has stood the test of time. Very advanced when first produced, and the winner of many endurance races, it still powers one of the world's finest motor cars in its present refined and developed form. As always the Jaguars were superb pieces of engineering, devoid of any gimmickry. In contrast, Mercedes were fielding a team of three new race cars equipped with all sorts of weird devices, including a swing rear axle, a design carried over from their production cars. Even then, this arrangement was a dangerous and outmoded form of rear suspension for a racing car.

The Le Mans track had not kept pace with the development of racing sports cars, and the pit area alongside a fast narrow straight was a dangerous area for mechanics. It was during this Le Mans race of 1955 that the tragic accident occurred on this straight, in which over 80 people were killed and many more injured. Levegh, the driver of the Mercedes involved, was killed and the 100 S was put out of the race. Mike Hawthorn went on to win in the D-Type Jaguar.

Not too many people have had the experience of driving a 100 S in its prime, as only 55 were built. Without any doubt, it handled better than all the other big Austin Healey models, due to its lightness, near perfect weight distribution, and the sheer hard development work on the suspension and steering. Though somewhat limited in maximum rpm the engine had a wide band of power and acceleration was excellent up to over 100 mph. Due to the light loading and the high efficiency Burman steering gear, the car could be steered very precisely making it delightful to drive on twisty roads. The handling was markedly superior to the early cars with their 16-inch tyre and wheel equipment. Of course, the small section Dunlop 5.50-15 racing tyres had nothing like the grip of modern fat section tyres and rubber compounds.

Production of 100 S cars had continued at the Cape works throughout 1955, the last one to be built, No. 3804, being shipped to Ed Bussey in Florida in November. Six cars were sent direct to Australia and New Zealand but later on many more used 100 Ss were bought and shipped out to that continent, including the car bought by Mintex for use in developing pad materials. Lionel Clegg of Mintex was a frequent visitor to Warwick, and a good customer for discs until they became available in cast iron. At the time, there were fears that cast iron would not stand up to the high temperatures and would crack but these later proved unfounded. In fact, the stability of cast iron discs eliminated coning and consequent high pedal travel in a well used car. Mike Sharp, now a Barford resident, eventually bought the Mintex car which Dick Protheroe maintained and raced with much success in England.

After the end of production, the development of the works 100 S cars continued, with the use of two twin choke carburettors to improve mixture distribution and power output. Using the highlift long period camshafts with two 2-inch SUs gave over 140 bhp; fitting two 45 DCOE Webers, with the same engine specification, raised this to 145 bhp and greatly improved the output at lower engine speeds. The front suspension was improved using the later pattern of stub axles and lower links, with a heavier section

Tommy Wisdom trying out a works 100 S at the USAAF base at Brize Norton, Oxfordshire.

anti-roll bar. We put a lot of effort into reducing the weight of the cars. A tubular steel four-branch exhaust manifold replaced the lump of iron used on the production Ss, and a few remaining steel body parts were replaced with light alloy. These cars scaled 1,790 lb with 53 per cent of the weight on the rear wheels. They handled well and were very quick. The engines would run up to 6,000 rpm with apparent reliability, but since the power dropped appreciably beyond 5,500 rpm this was set as the safe rpm limit.

We entered two of those special 100 Ss in the 1956 Sebring 12-hour race. After seven hours, the first car, driven by Lance Macklin and Archie Scott Brown, was lying in eighth position when the exhaust manifold broke up. The second car, driven by Roy Jackson Moore and Forbes-Robinson, also retired with a similar failure. The long stroke S units were rough when run to high rpm and this caused the break-up of the exhaust manifolds. With the failure of the works cars, the Austin Healey contingent was reduced to one, Ed Bussey's 100 S driven by Phil Stiles and George Huntoon, and they finished eleventh.

One odd car was developed into an S mechanical specification coupé. This was a red 100 with a fixed top styled by Gerry Coker. It was modified in Austin's experimental body shop and on its return to Warwick became

A preliminary rendering for the coupé 100. This was developed into the red and black car used by DMH, which evolved into an S specification.

DMH's personal car until 1962. The first improvement was the fitting of Dunlop disc brakes. It next had the 100 S chassis modification added, including Armstrong rear dampers with electrically operated ride control. A 100 S power unit was then rebuilt, with an overdrive added to the gearbox.

The addition of the fixed metal top greatly increased the rigidity of the whole car, and with various suspension modifications resulted in better roadholding and greater ride comfort. Most of its early life was concentrated on brake development and general development as an addition to the model range. The S engine gave the vehicle excellent performance and fuel consumption, but it could be hot and uncomfortable in hot weather, despite additional insulation, sound deadening and air ducting.

DMH and I put in many miles on this coupé, including a trip to Italy when Stirling Moss and DMH carried out a recce of the Mille Miglia circuit. I once put it through a hedge into a field with very little damage: after a little attention to the body, it was possible to continue with the testing. By good fortune this car eventually went to a good home where Arthur Carter now keeps it in a manner better than that to which it had become accustomed.

The S engine was seriously considered as a replacement for the 90 hp 100 engine. In the 1950s, the greatest sales competitor faced by the 100 was the Triumph TR series. The Triumph engine was a very efficient unit, returning

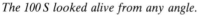

The 100 S looked alive from any angle.

extremely good fuel consumption, and a great deal of effort went into research and development with S engined cars in an attempt to better the Triumph results. S engine development finally ceased with the arrival of the new six-cylinder BMC engine, the 'C' series, as this had to be fitted in as many models as possible in order to obtain the advantages of volume production.

Austin Healey 100 S
Specification

ENGINE: Bore 3.4375 in (87.3 mm); stroke 4.375 in (111.1 mm); capacity 162.2 cu in (2660 cc); bhp 132 at 4,700 rpm; maximum torque 168 lb ft at 2,500 rpm; compression ratio 8.3:1; maximum bmep 157 lb/sq in at 2,500 rpm.

Cylinders: Four cylinders cast integral with crankcase. Full length water jackets. Aluminium alloy cylinder head with valve seat inserts.

Crankshaft: Forged-steel, counterbalanced crankshaft supported in three detachable steel-backed tri-metal bearings. Crankshaft nitride hardened.

Connecting Rods: Forged-steel with detachable steel-backed tri-metal big-end bearings. Fully floating wrist pin.

Pistons: Solid skirt type in low expansion aluminium alloy with aluminite finish. Two compression rings and one oil control ring fitted.

Camshaft: High-lift forged-steel, supported in three detachable steel-backed white-metal bearings. Cams of patented design for quiet operation. Driven by Duplex roller chain from crankshaft with oil catchers to maintain chain lubrication.

Valves: Overhead valves operated by push-rods. Large inlet valves of silicon chrome steel; exhaust valves 'KE.965' steel designed to resist corrosion from leaded fuels.

Lubrication: Pressure gear pump forces oil to all main, big-end, camshaft and overhead-valve rocker-shaft bearings. Holes in the big-end bearings provide for jet lubrication of the cylinder walls, and the front camshaft bearing provides a controlled feed of oil to the timing chain. Both main and big-end bearing oil feeds are of patented design which ensures longer crankshaft life. A full-flow oil cooler with renewable filter element is fitted. Oil capacity approximately 20 imp pints. 24 US pints.

Cooling: Circulation by centrifugal type of pump. Fan-cooled pressurised radiator. Water is directed to sparking plug bosses and exhaust port walls. Cooling system capacity 20 pints (24 US pints).

Fuel System: Fuel from a rear tank of 20 imp gallons (24 US gallons) capacity is fed by two SU large capacity electrical pumps to twin SU carburettors fitted with cold air intake pipe.

Exhaust: High efficiency twin-pipe system.

Ignition: Coil and battery ignition with automatic advance and retard and additional vacuum control.

Dynamo: 12-volt fan-ventilated unit with compensated voltage control.

Starter: Operated by push-button solenoid type switch.

CLUTCH: Flexible dry single-plate Borg and Beck clutch is fitted, with spring cushion drive. Clutch diameter 10 in. Specially constructed for racing.

GEARBOX: Four forward speeds and reverse controlled by a short central gear lever and with synchromesh engagement for top, 3rd and 2nd gears. Oil capacity 5 imp pints, 6 US pints.

PROPELLER SHAFT: Hardy Spicer propeller shaft with needle roller bearing universal joints. Lubrication nipples to each joint.

REAR AXLE: Spiral bevel three-quarter floating in a banjo-type casing. The pinion is carried by pre-loaded taper roller bearings. Oil capacity $2\frac{1}{2}$ pints (1.29 litres.) Normal ratio 2.92, alternative ratios availabe 3.66:1, 4.125 and 2.69.

OVERALL GEAR RATIOS: 8.98, 5.57, 3.88 and 2.92 with 12.2 reverse.

STEERING: Burman cam and lever steering gear. Adjustable steering wheel with aluminium alloy spokes and wooden rim.

Brian's cap and the Austin in the background were typical of the time. He now uses the cap to keep the paint out of his hair when creating his masterpieces of Cornish seascapes.

SUSPENSION: Front – independent coil springs controlled by double-acting Armstrong RXP hydraulic shock absorbers interconnected by an anti-roll torsion bar. Rear – semi-elliptic springs controlled by double-acting Armstrong RXP hydraulic shock absorbers and anti-sway bar.

BRAKES: Dunlop disc brakes on front and rear wheels. Handbrake operates on rear discs only.

WHEELS AND TYRES: Wire-spoke knock-on wheels with 5.50 × 15 Dunlop racing tyres. Quick-lift jacking points and racing jack.

ELECTRICAL: One 12-volt 38 AH battery; positive earth; built-in side- and twin tail-lamps; twin horns; Le-Mans type headlamps. Spark plugs Champion NA.10.

INSTRUMENTS: Fuel gauge; oil pressure, oil temperature and water temperature gauges; 140 mph speedometer; 0–6,000 rpm tachometer.

COACHWORK: Open two-seater with individual bucket seats; all-aluminium body; one-piece perspex screen.

OVERALL DIMENSIONS: Wheelbase 7 ft 6 in; track and front 4 ft 1⅝ in; track at rear 4 ft 2¾ in; overall length 12 ft 4 in; overall width 5 ft 0½ in; height over scuttle 2 ft 11⅞ in; height over windshield 3 ft 6 in; ground clearance 5½ in; turning circle 35 ft.

WEIGHT: Dry 1,888 lb.
     Kerb water, oil and 5 gallons petrol – 1988 lb.

Performance Data: Piston Area 37.2 sq in. Top gear mph per 1,000 rpm – 26.6.

ENGINE:

Number of Cylinders	4
Bore	3.4375 in (87.3 mm)
Stroke	4.375 in (111.1 mm)
Capacity	162.2 cu in (2,660 cc)
Brake Horse Power	130 at 4,700 rpm
Max Torque	168 lb/ft at 2,500 rpm
Compression Ratio	8.4:1
Firing Order	1, 3, 4, 2
Valves	Overhead, push rod operated, double springs
Valve Timing: Inlet Opens	10° btdc
Inlet Closes	50° abdc
Exhaust Opens	45° bbdc
Exhaust Closes	15° atdc
Valve Clearance (cold)	.015 in
Lift	.435 in

LUBRICATION:

Pump	Straight gear or rotor
Running Pressures	50/55 lb per sq in
Sump Capacity	20 imp pints: 24 US pints
Filter	Full flow

FUEL SYSTEM:

Carburettors	Twin SU H6
Pump	2 SU Electric
Model	LCS High Pressure
Tank Capacity	20 imp gal; 24 US gal

COOLING SYSTEM:

Circulation	Pump and fan
Capacity	20 imp pints; 24 US pints

IGNITION:

Coil	Lucas B12
Distributor	Lucas DM2
Contact Breaker Gap	.014–.016 in
Timing	6° btdc
Sparking Plugs	NA.10
Plug Gap	.025 in

CLUTCH:

Make	Borg and Beck
Type	Single dry plate
Diameter	10 in
Withdrawal Bearing	Self lubricating carbon ring

GEARBOX:

Number of Gears	4 forward; 1 reverse
Gear Ratios: 1st	3.08 (1)
2nd	1.91 (2)
3rd	1.33 (3)
Top	Direct
Oil Capacity	$4\frac{1}{2}$ pints; 5.35 US pints

PROPELLER SHAFT:

Make	Hardy Spicer
Type	Open shaft; needle roller brgs

REAR AXLE:

Type	Spiral bevel
Oil Capacity	$2\frac{1}{4}$ imp pints; 2.7 US pints
Overall Gear Ratios:	
1st Gear	8.98
2nd Gear	5.57
3rd Gear	3.88
Top Gear	2.92
Reverse	12.2

STEERING:

Type	Burman Cam and Lever
Ratio	12.6:1
Steering Wheel Diameter	$16\frac{1}{2}$ in
Turning Circle	35 ft 0 in
Toe-in	$\frac{1}{16}-\frac{1}{8}$ in

Brian, the good looking member of the family, with his hat at the right angle.

SUSPENSION:

Front	Independent: coil spring
Rear	Semi-elliptic leaf spring
Shock Absorber – front & rear	Armstrong double acting hydraulic RXP
Stabiliser – front	Anti-roll torsion bar
rear	Anti-sway bar

BRAKES:

Make	Dunlop
Type	Hydraulic disc
Handbrake	Mechanical, rear wheels only

WHEELS:

Type	Wire spoked
Hub	Knock-on cap

TYRES:

Size	5.50 × 15 Racing
Pressure: front (normal)	28 lb/sq in
rear (normal)	32 lb/sq in

CHASSIS:

Type	Integral body and frame
Frame	Box section – cross bracing

ELECTRICAL EQUIPMENT:

Battery	1 × 12-volt positive earth
Capacity	38 amp hr at 10 hr rate
Dynamo	Lucas type C.39 PV2
Starter	Lucas type M.418.G
Cut-out and Regulator	Lucas type RB.106
Fuse Unit	Lucas type SF.6

141

The following table gives the relationship between engine speed and road speed in the various gears. These figures are based on the Dunlop 5.50 × 15 racing tyres at 32 lb/sq in rear pressure and 2.92 axle ratio:

ROAD SPEED		ENGINE RPM		
mph	1st	2nd	3rd	Top
10	1155	716	499	375
20	2310	1432	997	750
30	3465	2148	1496	1125
40	4620	2865	1995	1500
50		3581	2494	1875
60		4297	1992	2250
70		5013	3491	2625
80			3990	3000
90			4489	3375
100			4987	3750
110				4125
120				4500
130				4875
140				5250

HAND CONTROLS:

Hand Brake: Situated on the right-hand side of the propeller shaft tunnel, between the seats. To release, pull rearwards slightly and depress button, then push forward fully. Operates on rear wheels only.

Gear Lever: Should always be left in neutral when starting the engine. The lever is mounted on the left side of the gearbox. To engage a gear, depress the clutch and move the lever to the required position.

Choke Control: Located on the left of the steering, underneath the fascia. For use when the engine is cold. Pull out to limit until the engine fires, and return it to the half-way position for rapid warming up. The choke must be fully released at the earliest moment possible.

Ignition Switch: Turn the key clockwise to switch on. Do not leave the switch 'on' when the vehicle is stationary – the warning light is a reminder. The ignition key may also be used for locking the luggage compartment.

Lighting Switch: Mounted above the ignition switch. Pull out to put on sidelights; twist to right and pull again to put on headlights. The headlights are dipped by foot operation.

Starter Switch: Press in the control to start, and release as soon as the engine fires. If the engine fails to start after a few revolutions, do not operate the starter again until the engine is stationary.

Panel Light Switch: Slide the switch to the right to illuminate the instruments. Only operates when the sidelights are 'on'.

Air Intake Control: A supply of cold air can be admitted to the car interior for ventilating purposes by pulling out the control on the left-hand side of the car. The cold air is directed into the right-hand foot well.

Horn Button: Mounted at the centre of the steering wheel; operated independently of the ignition switch.

Steering Column Adjustment: The steering column may be adjusted to give the most suitable steering wheel position. To raise or lower the steering wheel, first release the locking ring immediately behind the steering wheel hub. Slacken this locking ring two or three turns in a clockwise direction, move the steering wheel up or down as desired, then re-lock in the new position.

Bonnet: The bonnet is secured by two hooks and a strap. To open bonnet, lift hooks and turn 180° then undo one side of strap only. There is a rod to hold bonnet in open position.

OPERATING INSTRUCTIONS:
New cars direct from Factory.

The car is road tested and part run-in. The engine is filled with SAE.20 oil. This oil should be changed at 500 miles and the engine filled with a recommended oil. The normal Austin Healey 500-mile check should be carried out.

The engine is built with racing clearances and it will be noisier than standard engines. Do not reduce valve clearance in an attempt to reduce noise. The correct clearance of .015 inches must be maintained.

Alan 'Sebring' Jones, a leading Australian 100 S exponent and authority, restored this car shortly before he was killed whilst helping others. (George Goodacre)

Healey: The Specials

The special equipment available for the Austin Healey '100' (Model BNI) is not suitable for the Austin Healey 100 S.

The Dunlop disc brakes are covered by a separate leaflet.

The quicklift racing jack is designed for racing use. Under the nose and tail of the car there are two jack locating points. Assemble the jack and roll it under the car and locate the top rail in the location points. Then pull the handle to the ground: this raises the end of the car for wheel changing. A bottle screw jack is provided in the tool kit for normal use.

Front wheel bearings are of the Timken tapered roller type. Adjust as follows:

Relieve the bearings of all load by raising the wheel from the ground.

Remove the hub cap and cotter pin.

Tighten up the adjusting nut whilst rotating the wheel in both directions until a slight bind is felt indicating that all the surfaces of the bearings are in contact.

Back off the adjusting nut ⅙ to ¼ of a turn or sufficiently to allow the wheel to rotate freely without excessive end play. Recommended end play .004–.006 inch.

Lock the adjusting nut, ensuring that the bearing adjustment is not disturbed.

It was always cold and foggy in Warwick when we got the cars ready to ship them to Sebring. The labels on the windowshields were for shipping.

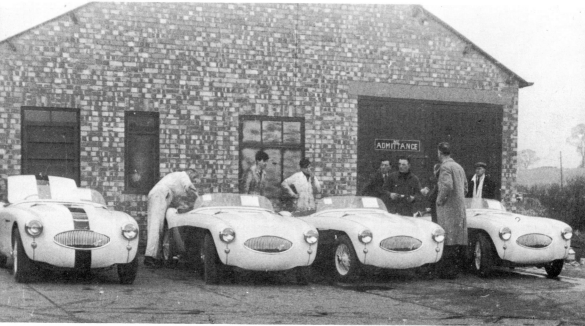

A slight rock will be perceptible at the wheel rim or edge of brake disc, which should not be confused with slackness in the swivel pins.

Oil filter should be removed and element changed every 15,000 miles.

Do not overstrain the banjo bolts and always use good washers.

February 1955.

INSTRUMENTS:
Speedometer: Registers the vehicle speed and total mileage. The trip figures at the top of the speedometer can be set to zero by pushing up the knob at the bottom of the speedometer and turning it to the right.

Tachometer: This instrument indicates the revolutions per minute of the engine and thus assists the driver in determining the most effective engine speed range for maximum performance in any gear.

Oil Pressure Gauge: Indicates the oil pressure in the engine. It does not show the quantity of oil in the sump.

Ignition Warning Light: Glows red when the ignition is switched 'on' and fades out when the dynamo is charging the battery.

Headlight Beam Warning Light: A red light appears when both headlights are switched on, with the two beams full ahead. The light goes out when the headlights are dipped.

Fuel Gauge: Indicates the contents of the petrol tank when the ignition is switched on. When the tank is being filled switch off to stop engine, switch on again and the needle will record the amount of fuel entering the tank.

Water Temperature Gauge: This records the temperature of the cooling water circulating in the cylinder block and radiator.

Fuel Reserve Switch and Warning Light: The lower left hand switch controls the switching of the pumps. Operation of the reserve pump is indicated by the green light in the centre of the panel.

Oil Temperature Gauge: Records the temperature of the oil in the sump. The oil then passes through the cooler and is delivered to the bearings at a lower temperature.

Battery Master Switch: This switch is located in the engine compartment.

FOOT CONTROLS:
Accelerator: The right pedal.

Brakes: The centre pedal which operates the hydraulic brakes on all four wheels.

Clutch: The left pedal. Do not rest the foot on this pedal when driving, and do not hold the clutch out to 'free wheel'.

Dip Switch: If the headlights are on full, a touch on the foot dip switch alters the lights to the 'dipped' position and they remain so until another touch returns them to 'full on'.

Into the Glorious Sixties

The six-cylinder engine replaced the A90-based four in the Austin Healey and in all the BMC large cars. The development of these six-cylinder Austin Healeys and the majority of the specials had already been covered in my first book, *Austin Healey: The Story of the Big Healeys*.

The first of the standard-bodied sixes, UOC 741, was to become the link between the Warwick-built competition cars and the Abingdon-built rally cars. Originally prepared and developed for competition use, at Warwick, at the instigation of DMH's old friend, Tommy Wisdom, it subsequently went to Abingdon to become the first of their rally Healeys. UOC 741 incorporated the 100 S strengthening gussets and larger rear dampers, and complete details of these were passed on to Marcus Chambers, who then ran BMC's not too successful competition department. From then on two different lines of competition vehicles developed. We concentrated on producing light cars for competition in long distance races. In contrast, the Abingdon cars were much heavier with an emphasis on strength to enable them to carry two men over rough terrain at high speed.

At the Cape works we did not have any panel beaters for many years and we therefore subcontracted all bodywork to outside firms. This was not entirely satisfactory and it was also very expensive. A lot of this subcontract

An open form of a proposed six cylinder, showing an alternative outlet for hot air. Contrary to general opinion, we did try hard to reduce cockpit heat.

Another Gerry Coker rendering of what might have been the six cylinder. We went as far as producing the wooden buck to form the skin panels. Headlamp treatment would have been a problem in US form.

The 'L' type: a body styling drawing for a longer wheel base Healey with improved rear seats. The project was cancelled when we produced the BN4 configuration.

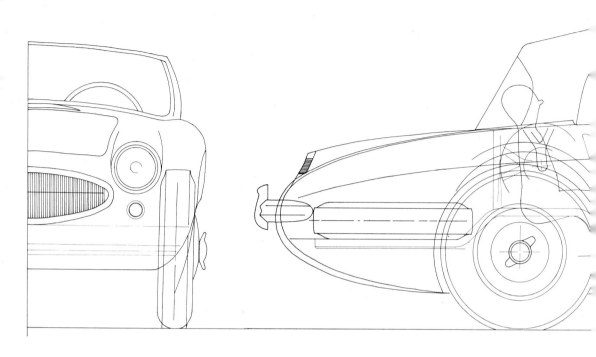

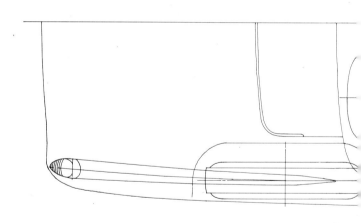

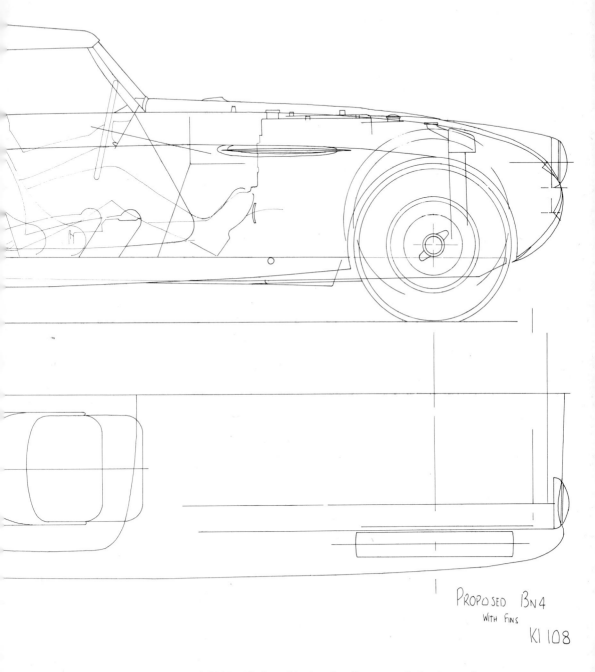

PROPOSED BN4
WITH FINS
KI 108

A line drawing of a proposed BN4 with fins. Meeting headlamp regulations was always a problem on a small car and this was a possible solution.

work was carried out by Bill Buckingham who finally agreed to join us full-time – a stroke of luck, as he was the best panel beater in the district. He was later joined by young Terry Westwood who showed a natural aptitude for the work, including a flair for welding aluminium panels. Bill did all the panel work on all the Sebring and Le Mans Sprites and on the SR/XR37 race car, plus various modifications of Sprite bodywork.

Les Ireland developed the system we used to build special bodies quickly. First a quarter-size drawing of the body lines would be drawn, with very accurate cross sections every 10 inches. These cross sections would be 'blown up' to full size and reproduced on plywood. The plywood sections were then mounted on an accurate solid wooden base. Other sections would be produced as required and fitted to the wooden buck. Bill Buckingham would then produce the skin by panel beating a number of pieces and welding them together to fit. Finally, the welds would be hammered and filed smooth. Special understructures were built up as the result of sheet metal modifications to production frames, this work being handled by Roger Menadue and Jim Cashmore. By this system we were able to produce light alloy racing bodies quickly and at comparatively low cost.

At the Cape works we were also concerned with producing high-speed motor boats. Contructed of marine ply and powered by marinized BMC engines, these boats performed well and had a good reputation. We later produced boats made of glass reinforced plastic, which gave us the ability to make car bodies and parts in this material. Four bug-eye Sprites were produced with GRP bodies, from moulds taken off a highly finished production body. The resulting cars were very light and were used at Sebring in 1961. However, we were never really satisfied with the finish obtainable in this material, and after these four bodies used it only for seats and hardtops.

The Cape was always a very busy place, but its remoteness from the main street gave it certain disadvantages as a showroom which were blamed by the sales organization for their poor performance. When the derelict cinema in Coten End became available, we sold the Cape works and moved a larger retail organization combined with a condensed manufacturing unit into the modified cinema buildings. For a time the experimental shop shared the main building with an expanding service department. Under

UOC 741 with Cecil Winby, during scrutineering at the Mille Miglia. This was the first of many six-cylinder specials. (Photo taken by George Phillips of Autosport *at Brescia, 1957)*

BMC competition department's answer to the ground clearance problem on the 1967 RAC Rally Big Healey.

The first six cylinder competition car being prepared at the Cape, by Bill Hewitt and Tommy Wisdom.

The last special bodied race car to be built. This is a good example of the quality of the panel work carried out by Bill Buckingham.

these difficult conditions, we continued to produce special cars.

It was during this period that the first of the streamlined Sprites was produced. These cars were run at Sebring and Le Mans from 1965 to 1968. In the 1967 and 1968 Le Mans, the same car won the Motor Trophy for the highest placed all-British car. It has since ended up in a good home with Ian Polley. The first of this type, the original prototype, is now in the USA with Gary Kohs.

As the development of the six-cylinder cars continued, we produced some specials which looked normal but which were panelled throughout in light alloy, gaining considerably more performance through this reduction in weight. The first of these light alloy panel sets was made by hand by Bill Buckingham. BMC later produced alloy panels off the production tools for us and their competition department, which saved a lot of time and money.

One significant modification on the later cars was the reworking of the rear of the chassis frame, where it passed under the rear axle. This gained a useful increase in wheel movement. At the same time, torque arms were added to permit the use of lower rate rear springs. When the Austin Healey 100 was first designed, the spring design was based on a gross vehicle weight some 400 lb lighter and with 60 less bhp than the 3000. The spring length was limited by this original design and was too short to resist axle torque.

Two fixed head coupés were produced on a 3000 chassis. The first, X312, was built on to a modified Sebring chassis with its dropped rear frame members and torque arms and high output engine. DMH and I schemed a one-piece roof line and Doug Thorpe carried out the detailed design. A number of Bundy tubes were then welded up and positioned on the car to give the desired outline, the bodywork being carried out by Jensen at West

The front end was the same shape as on the Sebring and Le Mans cars, with two of the four headlights omitted to save weight.

Bromwich. The engine was a rebuilt Sebring race engine, with an aluminium alloy head, full race camshaft, 11.5 to 1 compression ratio, light steel flywheel and four-speed close-ratio gearbox, with straight cut gears plus Laycock overdrive. The carburettors were three 1¾inch HD6 SUs on cast manifolds, with ¾-inch balance pipes and a progressive throttle mechanism that kept the throttles synchronised throughout the full operating range. The power output was down to 170 bhp at 5,300 rpm but the fuel consumption was very good, returning 20–24 mpg under normal use.

Stylist's renderings for the six-cylinder coupé. This car was developed as the 3000 S with the aim of forming a high priced addition to the Austin Healey range.

The rear of the car was modified to take a tank of a nominal 18 gallons capacity, giving a cruising range of 400 miles. Following competition practice, a roll-over bar was built in, forming a strong point for the attachment of the rear window which with its lifting surround gave access to a flat luggage platform. Peter Wilks of Rover tried the car and was very critical of the seats, proclaiming them to be uncomfortable and lacking in back support. Peter had a way of delivering a concise resumé of a car's defects that would silence the most pompous engineers. Needless to say, we listened and accepted his offer to have the Rover experts produce a pair of seats for us. Rover have always led the field in seat comfort and their experts quickly built a pair that gave support in all the right areas without any loss of headroom – a critical factor.

The car was heavier than the production 3000, with more weight on the rear axle, and suitable springs were selected from our stock of experimental parts. A heavy front anti-roll bar off a Rootes commercial vehicle was fitted at the front, using Armstrong shock-absorber links. At the rear we fitted DAS10 shock-absorbers with a remote four-position adjustment operated by levers on the propeller shaft tunnel. This gave a very hard setting for

Cockpit heat was always a problem with our cars. We tried a variety of outlets on the front wings and there were schemes for the six-cylinder coupé model. Vents in this position did reduce cockpit temperatures.

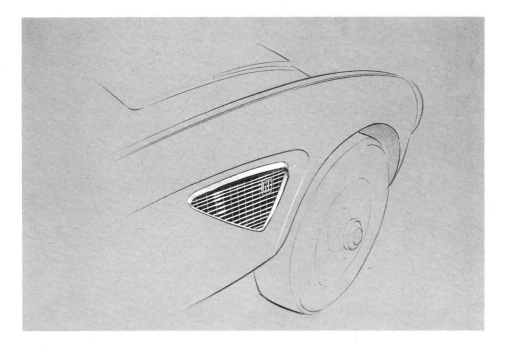

high speeds, and a very soft setting for crawling through towns. The car was equipped with all-round disc brakes – Girling type 16P at the front, and type 12/10 with handbrake at the rear. With their Mintex pads they provided excellent stopping power without fade or judder.

The car was intended to be an addition to the Austin Healey model range and not a replacement for the 3000 convertible. George Harriman was very keen to expand the Austin Healey range in this way and had Dick Burzi, Austin's talented stylist, look at the car and make some minor changes for production. In addition, Dick took an older car and built another simpler version of the concept. This involved fewer changes to the base model, with the addition of a completely new trim and seat style. Jensen were called in to provide detailed costs for the changes. Whilst their quoted cost per unit was acceptable, they also demanded a high tooling charge which Austin would not accept. I believe they may have misinterpreted Austin's interest, thinking they could recover the retooling costs of many existing parts in addition to the new panels. Austin had already spent a lot on tooling up for the MGB GT and MGC and reasoned that a common Austin Healey/MG model would be a more sensible approach. The project accordingly died.

We purchased the second Austin styled coupé, while the original coupé was mainly used by DMH and myself. Its appearance caused much favourable comment and it was a very fast long-distance car, with its excellent handling and comfort. Both cars have now ended up in a good home with Don Humphries of the Austin Healey Club Midland Centre, who is carrying out a first rate restoration.

The six cylinder coupé prototype produced by Austin and styled by Dick Burzi of Austin.

The Austin styled coupé. This second prototype was a development of the first Warwick design, having fewer panel changes and using normal Austin Healey bumpers.

Interior of the Austin styled coupé, showing the specially trimmed seats with integral head restraints. The interior trim was to a very high standard.

The 3000 coupé at Austin for the production study. This car had a slightly shorter tail. Wing side vents did help to reduce the underbonnet temperature.

The streamlined Sprite car in bare metal, whilst being constructed at the cinema in Warwick. We made a few jigs and fixtures for these, including the cradle which picked up on holes in the chassis frame.

Engine troubles with the early 100 Six race cars prompted us to look around for an alternative power unit. Peter Collins, a leading Grand Prix and sports car driver, was a good friend of DMH and he suggested that we used a Ferrari 2.5 litre engine. He then went one stage further and arranged for us to purchase a complete car from the Marquis de Portago. This car was somewhat sick after a good racing career, but with Austin's help its engine was stripped and rebuilt with new pistons to run on petrol. Austin were not disinclined to examine in detail what had been a leading racing engine, for with its claimed 210 bhp it should have made a highly competitive sports car unit.

X224: a modified 100 S chassis fitted with the Ferrari Grand Prix engine.

X224 was based on a modified S chassis fitted with the long nose six-cylinder race body that had been developed from the 1956 record breaker. Roger Menadue and Jim Cashmore carried out most of the modifications necessary to fit the Ferrari engine and rear axle suspension assembly. We used MGA rack and pinion steering. Barry Bilbie had the task of determining the exact position in which to fit the rack for the best steering geometry. Quite a lot of drawing office time was spent on this layout, as we viewed rack and pinion as a possible improvement to the Austin Healey steering.

Essentially a short distance Grand Prix engine, the Ferrari unit was not really satisfactory because of its high rate of oil consumption. Peter Collins drove the car at Nassau in the series of races they used to run in December as a tourist attraction. It displayed a voracious appetite for oil and he had to make a pit stop for replenishment.

X224 at the rear of the Cape works. The sheds were used for storing experimental bits and pieces, most of which were sent to a local scrap merchant when the factory was sold.

Eddie Maher and Jack Goffin at Morris Engines, Coventry subsequently made considerable progress in developing the six-cylinder Austin Healey unit into a racing power plant. We replaced the Ferrari engine with this 175 hp unit, and despite the increase in weight, the car became a lot quicker: the Coventry horses were certainly very strong. Roy Salvadori drove it in the next Nassau races, achieving second place in one, and retiring with an oil-soaked clutch in another.

X224 was eventually dismantled and scrapped, the Ferrari bits being returned to the Grand Prix car which was sold. As a competition project, this had not been a success, but it was an interesting development exercise and helped widen the team's knowledge of motor cars.

The Sprite/Midget model was the subject of considerable attention in the search for a suitable model to follow it. The cars were selling well, filling that important low-cost sector of the market. Any alterations to the fully tooled body produced by Pressed Steel would be expensive, and although Austin had thoughts of a new car they were not sure what it should be. Alec Issigonis – Austin's technical director, Charles Griffin, Syd Enever and I had a meeting at which a strategy was laid down. Austin would build a prototype using their well proven transverse front-wheel-drive layout, MG would build one with a conventional front-engine, rear-drive configuration, and we would build one with the transverse engine at the rear, with hydrolastic suspension. Austin thus had to attempt to control the efforts of three prototype units simultaneously, and although three different machines finally evolved, none went further than working prototypes, none of which could be called a sports car.

A scheme for a four-seater on an Austin 1100 base. This later evolved into the WAEC car with the transverse-mounted Cooper 'S' unit at the rear.

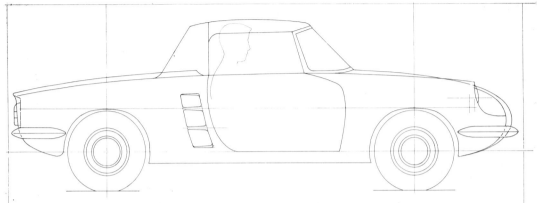

A line drawing of WAEC, a two-seater prototype with the transverse BMC unit at the rear.

DMH next had an idea for a 3000 replacement. The 'C' series engine, now developed into a powerful, reliable but heavy power unit, was due to be dropped from production. This was primarily because the United States authorities had released details of proposed legislation that would be extremely difficult to meet without making extensive modifications. In fact, many of the most difficult regulations were dropped from the final requirements, after many manufacturers had spent a great deal of time and money in complying with them. Meanwhile, Austin were producing a new model, the Princess R, fitted with a Rolls-Royce engine. With overhead inlet and side exhaust valves, this was a light alloy six-cylinder unit, known as the FB, designed and developed specifically for motor cars and not to be confused with the somewhat similar units built for military use. With just under 4 litres displacement, these units delivered 170 bhp quietly and very smoothly and they were much lighter than the 3000 engine. Austin were committed to take a large number of these engines and the idea of using it in a sports car interested them.

We obtained drawings and one unit from Austin and produced installation drawings. One proposed regulation would have required an increase in the interior width of the 3000. By using an Austin car axle, we would obtain an increase of 6 inches in the track, and so we decided to widen the body by 6 inches. A completed body was set up on stands and a line scribed down the centre. The body was cut up with a hacksaw and the two halves set up 6 inches apart. Pieces to join the two halves were then cut and welded in position. The sheet metal skin had pieces let in and the surface metal was finished to avoid the use of filler. We modified a steering column to incorporate the AC Delco safety unit with two universal joints, which gave an improved seating to steering wheel relationship. The springs and shock absorber settings were identical to those used on the production 3000 and the standard 3000 grille was retained. We built this first car with automatic transmission. The ride and handling qualities were superior to those of the 3000. Whereas the 'C' series engine would become rough at high engine speed, the Rolls-Royce unit was completely smooth and quiet throughout the speed range. Despite greater frontal area and comfort, the performance was as good as on the 3000.

The heavier bumper section and improved rear lamps help to distinguish what would have been the 4000.

The Rolls-Royce engine in Peter Cox's car. The six inch insert can be seen in the centre of the bulkhead.

The first Rolls-Royce engined prototype as it is today, completely restored by Peter Cox.

Peter Cox's restored 4000 prototype.

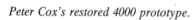

We duly presented this car to Austin. They liked the concept and agreed a design and development programme for six cars, under the code number ADO 24. This work was to be carried out in close co-operation with MG, who would have been responsible for quantity production. However, at the end of April 1967, Austin cut the programme to two vehicles, and they later killed the project entirely. BMC were now joined with Jaguar in a company called British Motor Holdings, and the decision was probably prompted by a reassessment of the combined model range, where both Jaguar and Austin Healey models competed in a similar sector. In fact, cutting one particular model from a range does not necessarily result in those remaining picking up more sales. In this case, as so often happened, it was the Japanese who picked up most of the slack.

The three prototypes were sold and the first has since been rebuilt and restored by Peter Cox of the South-western Centre of the Austin Healey Club. It is most gratifying that club members have rescued so many of the special cars in this way, which might otherwise have gone to the scrap heap.

SR and XR 37

For the 1968 racing season, BMC again supported our efforts in a racing programme which would concentrate on the Sprites. DMH thought that it was time we had a go at something better than a high placing in a class at Le Mans, and we discussed the possibilities of building a real sports racing car, something that would finish with a high overall position. First we needed an engine giving some real horsepower and so we looked around for something suitable within the BMC group. Coventry Climax had produced a number of V8 racing engines which had won a great number of races and Formula One championships, before becoming obsolete when the Formula One capacity limit was increased to 3 litres. Leonard Lee of Climax had supported British racing efforts for many years and he typically agreed to lend us a 2-litre V8, and to support it with help from Wally Hassan and Harry Spears. This unit gave 240 bhp and seemed ideally suited to our project.

We first looked at the possibility of using a front-engined, rear drive layout, based on a sprite frame with considerable modifications. We soon dropped this in favour of a mid-engined car, as this offered so many advantages regarding weight, distribution, more even distribution of braking, and of couse superior road holding. Barry Bilbie and I drew this up very quickly around a sheet steel centre section and we persuaded John Thompsons to make us a couple of these. We then added the front and rear

I'M BACKING HEALEY. Brian Healey created this publicity decal.

suspensions to this very accurate centre piece. The rear suspension was typical of a sports racing car, being rose jointed and fully adjustable. Geometry changes were possible with the provision of alternative mounting points. The hub carriers were welded up out of sheet steel, a practice often followed in the USA. The front suspension was by unequal wishbones and coil springs. At both ends we had alternative anti-roll bar fixings, to enable us to vary the degree of roll stiffness. Cam Gears supplied a modified MGB steering rack.

The sheet steel understructure of SR.

For the braking system we naturally consulted our old friends at Girling, and their competition manager, Tony Cross, masterminded the supply of components. The Girling-designed discs of cast iron were mounted on the hubs by means of a system known as the Redmayne joint. This Girling arrangement, whilst positively locating the disc, eliminated the constraint of the normal design that imposed stresses on the disc and gave rise to distortion. Brake operation was by way of two light alloy hydraulic cylinders, operated by an adjustable balance bar. Most of the machining work was carried out by Bramwell and Whitehead in nearby Leamington Spa. These brakes proved to be excellent and never gave us any problems. Dunlop produced some Elektron alloy wheels with the centre lock, five-peg-drive system which carried their well known racing tyres.

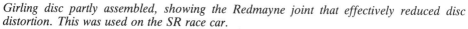

Girling disc partly assembled, showing the Redmayne joint that effectively reduced disc distortion. This was used on the SR race car.

We obtained a Hewland DG300 gearbox which incorporated the crown wheel and pinion final drive. The straight cut spur gears could easily be changed to provide a vast selection of gear ratio combinations for its five speeds. The gearbox was coupled to the engine using an AP twin plate competition clutch, again a well proven and excellent piece of equipment.

Barry Bilbie and Derek Westwood laid out the body lines which were reproduced in plywood sections for the body buck. Bernard Foster and Doug Green, the Barford builders, gave this object the benefit of their considerable wood-working skills. Using the wooden buck, Bill Buckingham and Terry Westwood then produced the sheet metal skin in Birmabright.

Smiths supplied us with a comprehensive set of their excellent instruments – a 0–10,000 rpm tachometer, oil pressure and temperature gauges, fuel pressure and water temperature gauges, plus an accurate fuel contents

The cockpit of SR.

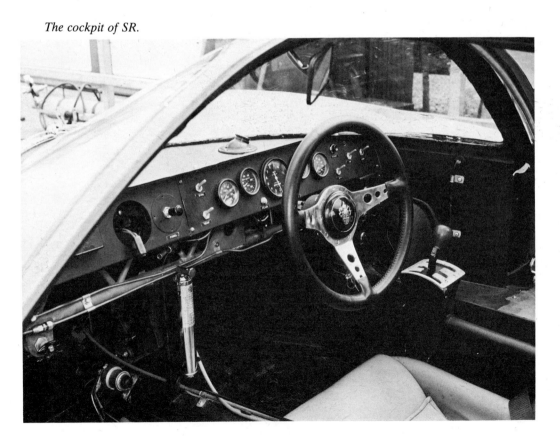

gauge. Lucas supplied every piece of electrical equipment and their competition manager, Ray Wood, organized the complete wiring of the vehicle. Lucas components are remarkably reliable and when they are responsible for wiring a vehicle, they leave nothing to chance. They are often unjustly blamed for component failures which, in 99 per cent of cases, are caused solely by faulty wiring by some ignorant yob. Wally Hassan advised us on the design of the oil system. This used an alloy oil tank, incorporating a simple but effective oil separator.

After a quick check and an immediate engine start, we took the machine to MIRA for some preliminary tests with John Harris. After a few gentle laps to warm it up, we changed the plugs to hard Champion racing plugs, and John gave it a real try-out. A racing Climax running up to 9,000 rpm makes a beautiful sound. After a few more laps, however, the engine went rough and John brought it in, saying that the clutch was behaving oddly. We found that the adapter plate between the gearbox and engine had broken. Although this adapter plate had been used successfully on many Formula One racing cars, it was now subject to greatly increased forces in a heavier sports car and would need major redesign. This was real trouble, as there was little time left before the Le Mans race. Wally Hassan again came to the rescue, modifying the cast oil sump to provide extra bolts at wider centres, and we fitted a new adapter plate machined out of a very high strength aluminium alloy.

After the rebuild and attention to other details, we conducted further tests at Silverstone with John Harris, Andrew Hedges and Clive Baker. Dunlop gave us read-outs on the tyre temperatures so that we could attempt to get the best grip out of the tyres. Initially, the car's handling was bad, but after some adjustments it was pronounced satisfactory although still capable of improvement. The whole process took time, especially as we seemed to be suffering unduly wet weather.

We used the Le Mans practice session for selecting the most suitable gear ratios. With the Climax performing superbly we were fairly confident of our chances. But during the race itself, disaster struck – just when Clive Baker had received the signal from our signallers at Mulsanne to come in for refuelling. The clutch jammed in the out position, effectively breaking the drive to the gearbox. That was the end of all our efforts. The clutch throw-out bearing had seized in the disengaged position and we did not free it until the unit was stripped at Climax.

Left: *SR in its original form with side-mounted radiators. It was finished in British racing green.*

SR loaded on the trailer for its first try-out at MIRA.

SR on the trailer and still in bare aluminium. The holes at the front were ducted to the brakes for cooling.

We obtained some comfort from the performance of the 1967 Sprite, which was now fitted with Lucas petrol injection. Driven by Roger Enever and Alec Poole, it finished 15th overall, taking the *Motor* Trophy for the second year in succession. After ten years of racing development, the Sprite was an extremely reliable and fast competition car, capable of 150 mph with its 1,293 cc BMC 'A' series engine. This 1968 Le Mans race was the last event in which a works Austin Healey would feature, for Lord Stokes was now in charge at BMC and had axed almost the entire Austin Healey programme.

We still had connections with the company as the Sprite was due to continue until 1970, and it was agreed that we could run SR at Le Mans in 1969. Leonard Lee again lent us a V8 Climax and we carried out detail modifications to increase the high speed stability and eliminate a trace of oversteer. Once again, we were to be unlucky. At an early stage of the race, the car got stuck in a jam caused by an accident. Racing cars do not use fans, depending on forward motion for cooling. The car overheated, causing a water leak to develop at the cylinder head joint, and this gave us no option but to withdraw it from the race.

Racing progress is such that the previous year's car is soon out of date, and for 1970 we had to make some radical changes. Regulations had changed in favour of open sports prototypes and so we decided to remove the heavy screen and top and generally improve the bodywork. In this respect we had some very helpful advice from Bill Heynes, now retired as a director of engineering at Jaguar, and Malcom Sayer, one of the industry's best men in the field of aerodynamics. With the lighter body structure we wanted an increased engine size and we contacted Peter Wilks about the possibility of using a tuned Rover unit – the light alloy Rover V8 was both powerful and reliable. Peter suggested that instead we looked around for a Repco Brabham 3-litre Formula One engine. This had the same origin as the Rover engine, being a development of the General Motors V8. Jack Brabham, Repco of Australia and Phil Irving had produced a powerful and very reliable 3-litre racing unit which for quite a long time had beaten the best European designs. My brother Bic duly approached Jack Brabham and he agreed to sell us an old engine suitably rebuilt for the Le Mans race. John Judd, one of the best engine builders, undertook this work, producing a unit that did all that was required without giving us a single problem. After the Le Mans race, John Judd rang me to see if he could buy the engine, as they were by then becoming very much sought after for hill climb cars. It

Overleaf: *John Harris and Jim Cashmore with SR at Silverstone – wet as usual.*

then transpired that Robert Harrison of Leyland Australia wanted the car without engine, the net result being that we had the use of the engine at Le Mans at very little cost.

The engine delivered to us was a Repco Brabham Formula One type RB740, number RB740/127E, and it gave the following power output:

276 bhp at 6,500 rpm
300 bhp at 7,000 rpm
306 bhp at 7,500 rpm
318 bhp at 8,000 rpm
322 bhp at 8,500 rpm

The Repco Brabham engine used in the 1970 Le Mans Healey, showing the unusual centrally placed exhaust system. It was rebuilt with a new AP twin plate clutch prior to its installation in XR37.

During the race, the maximum engine speed was limited to a very conservative 7,500 rpm, to ensure finishing. The bore and stroke were 3.5 and 2.37 inches respectively, with a capacity of 2,995 cc. The measured compression ratio was 11.5 to 1.

Tyre sizes had kept growing and on Dunlop's recommendation we increased the width of tyre fitted, necessitating wider rims front and rear. At the front we had 4.75/11.60 – 15 on 9-inch wide rims, and at the rear 5.75/13.60 – 15 on 12-inch rims. This final selection was a compromise between the high cornering power afforded by wide tyres and the lower power loss achieved with small-width tyres. Really wide tyres can reduce maximum speed when power is limited.

The Girling brakes were type 16/8/4 calipers with 12-inch diameter by 1.1-inch thick ventilated discs at the front, and BR calipers with $11.55 \times \frac{1}{2}$-inch thick solid discs at the rear, giving a 1 G retardation with a theoretical 138 lb of pedal pressure.

Lucas supplied all the electrical equipment, including their Opus ignition system, petrol injection system, alternator, lamps and battery.

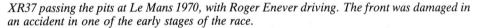

XR37 passing the pits at Le Mans 1970, with Roger Enever driving. The front was damaged in an accident in one of the early stages of the race.

John Harris did all the development testing at Gaydon and for the race itself the drivers were Roger Enever and Andrew Hedges. 1969 produced one of those wet Le Mans races. Before we had the word from Dunlop to fit their rain tyres, the car was involved in an accident with another competitor, necessitating some extensive front end body repairs. The special Dunlop rain tyres transformed the car's handling in the wet and the drivers were soon able to climb back up the field. They were again delayed when one of the dog clutches in the gearbox split in two pieces, requiring a gearbox rebuild. They continued to circulate the course on schedule and at the finish we were awaiting the arrival of the car at the end of its last lap. Our first thoughts were that Roger was taking a long time and we then learnt that he had broken down and could not restart the engine. After the race, Ray Wood found that a wire-wound resistor had broken due to vibration.

We went to Le Mans for the publicity. Our aim was to keep the Healey name in the public eye, for we were involved in producing a new production sports car which was released to public view at the Geneva Motor Show in 1972, as the Jensen Healey.

At the End:
A New Beginning

My brother Brian's health was not good and I disliked the retail side of the business. Gone were the Austin Healeys and gone was the special type of people who bought them. I was not unhappy to see the Donald Healey Motor Company sold by the family, since we retained Healey Automobile Consultants as a separate company, and this left me free to concentrate on the engineering side of the business. The Healey name also remained firmly in the family's control.

Jensen now built the Jensen Healey under agreement with Healey Automobile Consultants. Kjell Qvale had personally backed Jensen with a lot of money but the oil crisis and rising fuel costs all combined to bring about the end of the company. Its many problems were not made any easier by an attitude that seemed to prevail throughout the company, that Kjell would continue to pour money in regardless of what efforts were made to make profits. On 15th September 1975, an acute shortage of liquidity caused the directors to ask the Bank of America to appoint a receiver. A group, including DMH, strove to rescue the company and formulated a plan that was dependent upon £3 million from private sources and £2 million from the Government. This would have been sufficient to restructure the company and its model range, and would have returned it to good profitability within 18 months. Although the £3 million was available, the Government refused to supply the final £2 million. I simply cannot understand how the Government could later justify the application of over £50 million public money to enable a new company of foreign origin to make sports cars and employ a similar number of people. Maybe our hair was not long enough.

   Since the end of Jensen, we have been involved in a number of projects but it is possible to reveal the results of only a small number. DMH, who has always been something of an inventor, turned to the problem of alternative sources of energy and started investigating the use of a windmill as a means of generating power. He constructed a number of prototypes in

DMH and the windmill test rig bolted on to an old Mini pick up. This photo was taken during early testing at the wartime airfield at Perranporth.

Cornwall and succeeded in achieving a worthwhile output of power. A Mini pick-up was pressed into service as a mobile test bed, enabling machines to be tested at speeds up to 60 mph. He then tested several units under installed conditions on a Towermaster lattice tower. The final unit survived gale force winds of 80 mph, during which the tip speed of the blades exceeded the speed of sound, producing a noise audible over 2 miles away. This was during the tremendous storm that inflicted such heavy casualties upon the Fastnet ocean racers, when the whole of the British Isles received a terrible pounding. When the storm was at its height, I answered the phone to hear DMH shout, in a very excited voice, 'It stood up! It stood up!' At first I thought he meant his house. Despite a lot of interest in the project, demand was not sufficient to warrant putting it into production and it has been put to one side to await interest from an outside firm.

The quality of the Big Healeys displayed at US meetings is superb. It makes me feel many years younger.

We became involved with a number of sports car projects, only one of which has been revealed to the public. This was an exercise that we carried out in 1978 on a US specification Ford Fiesta. Many enthusiasts have lamented the demise of the Mini Cooper 'S', considering that the tarted-up substitutes subsequently offered by other manufacturers have missed the concept by a mile! An investigation showed that the basic 1600 cc US Fiesta was eminently suited for modification into a real flyer, and its Ford engine could be easily upgraded, using Mexico components, to give 100 bhp. We completed some styling drawings and an outline specification and submitted this to Detroit for approval.

A Fiesta was shipped over from the USA and we quickly stripped it out. We rebuilt the engine with new high compression pistons, a Mexico camshaft head, carburettors and manifolds, and the ultra high US final drive, which we replaced with the lower European ratio. All the parts used were production Ford components, readily available through dealers in England. A twin choke downdraught Weber carburettor, fitted with the stock Ford aircleaner, supplied the mixture. The engine was not run on a test bed, but a Ford Mexico engine in this state of tune, is known to develop over 105 bhp at 6,200 rpm, and the final test on a chassis dynamometer gave figures which indicated that this engine was giving a similar output.

We modified the suspension with different springs, roll bars and Koni adjustable shock absorbers, and fitted a set of 13-inch diameter Minilite wheels with 6-inch wide rims. We played around with various tyre equipment before deciding on Firestone BR60-13SS radials, which gave excellent grip on both dry and wet roads. The wheel arches were flared to provide wheel clearance and the body was finished in British racing green with pin striping to accentuate the form. The paint used was a stock Jaguar colour.

Road development was reduced to the minimum as the car was urgently required for show purposes, but even so it handled well and was a joy to drive. We would have loved to have kept it longer but Her Majesty's Customs and Excise had permitted us to import the car only for a specific purpose and a limited period. Pan American Airways collected it and flew it back to Detroit without damaging it in any way.

The car has been given a very good reception in the USA and has been displayed at many shows. In addition, *Road & Track*, one of the most influential motoring magazines, gave the car a road test and featured it on the front cover of their August 1979 issue, under the title 'Healey Fiesta, Fiesty, Fast and Fun.' Their editor-in-chief, Tony Hogg, gave it an excellent, detailed write up, concluding: 'Perhaps Ford will be able to persuade Donald Healey to work his magic on a legal but turbocharged version of the new Pinto – a project that would undoubtedly put a twinkle in

Donald Healey's eye, and also something that might turn out to be one of Ford's better ideas.'

Road & Track's world-wide circulation resulted in a lot of enquiries for copies of the car. We also received a couple of offers from other manufacturers for our services, but turned these down, not liking the countries or their products.

Currently we are involved in a number of car projects. One is the construction of a sports car for our own use, which is very much a spare-time job. The power plant is a Rover V8 with five-speed gearbox, fitted into a stark, light body. Only one car is being built, incorporating many original ideas with the aim of providing performance at a comparatively low cost. A body shape has been evolved that can be constructed without any

Bill Barnett sent me this photo of his car – one of many beautiful Healeys owned by club members in North America. The 1982 meeting should be sensational!

Overleaf: *An early layout for a personal sports car with a simple body construction. This project is now underway.*

compound curves. Our target date is 1982, when a meeting is being organized by the Austin Healey Club Pacific Center. The site selection has not been finalized: Aspen, Colorado is the prime choice but the Club says that Dallas and St Louis are also under consideration.

We always feared that the name would die when the Austin Healey went out of production, but today club membership is still expanding and annual gatherings like International Healey Day in England, the Austin Healey Club of America's Conclave, the Austin Healey Sports and Touring Club's Encounter and the Pacific Center's Austin Healey West, each result in around 300 assorted Healeys and their owners and other enthusiasts gathering together for fun and to exchange information. DMH and members of the family have enjoyed attending club meetings all over the world.

MG held their 50th anniversary celebrations at Abingdon in 1979, and now the MG marque is no longer produced. The sole surviving sports car available at an affordable price is the Triumph TR 7 convertible.

People sometimes ask why we don't restore a Healey. We started restoring a Bug Eye Sprite, but then sat back and thought, 'This is the wrong way to go – look ahead, innovate, build a new sports car!' Perhaps we will create something to replace the Austin Healey!

Appendix

Chassis and engine numbers of some of the Warwick-built special cars:

Build or Registration No.	Chassis No.	Engine No.	
AHX 1	BN1L 133237	1B136907	New York Show car
AHX 2	BN1L 133234	1B136892	California car
AHX 3	BN1L 133235	1B136899	DMH's car for US tour
AHX 4	BN1L 133236	1B136900	Geneva Show car
AHX 9	BN1 133238	1B136898	1st RH drive car
AHX 11	BN1L 134370	1B136788	Turin Show car
AHX 12	BN1L 134371	1B136913	
AHX 13	BN1L 134372	1B136912	
AHX 14	BN1L 134373	1B136869	
AHX 15	BN1L 134374	1B136915	
AHX 16	BN1 134375	1B139001	
AHX 17	BN1 134376	1B139002	Brake development car
AHX 18	BN1 134377	1B139006	
AHX 19	BN1 134378	1B136906	
AHX 20	BN1 134379	1B139003	

AHX 1953 Special Test Cars

NOJ 391	SPL 224B	1B136903	Mille Miglia and Le Mans
NOJ 392	SPL 225B	1B136876	Mille Miglia, later a test car with Girling disc brakes
NOJ 393	SPL 226B	1B136878	Le Mans
Not registered	SPL 227B	SPL 228B	24 Hour record car 1953 and 1954

100 S Cars (1954 Special Test Cars)

OON 439	SPL 256BN	SPL 256BN	Mille Miglia '54, '55, '56.
OON 440	SPL 257BN	SPL 257BN	Mille Miglia '54, and '55, Sebring '56
OON 441	SPL 258BN	SPL 258BN	Sebring '54, Mille Miglia '54 and '55
AHR 27	SPL 261BN	SPL 259BN	1954 Streamliner
		XSP 234–6	1956 Streamliner
NWD 977	BN3/4 S276	C26W 3902	6 cylinder prototype
Q1	H950Q1	2A1428HC EXP	1st Sprite prototype
Q2	H950Q2	———	2nd Sprite prototype
ST400/7080AC	AN5 14849	9CUH 14381	TFR1 1st Targa Florio Sprite
MARS		16GC-U-H-241	1622cc engined Sprite
UOC 741	BN4 51138	XSP 234–8	1st 100 Six rally car
ONX 113	BN1 142615	1B139174	Red and Black S Coupé
OAC 1	BN1 149458	1B139123	2nd Coupé: 6 cylinder engine fitted later

Experimental 'X' Numbers
X1 8 ft wheelbase 2 seater (Red Bug)
X2 Prototype Silverstone
X3 Prototype with Morris Minor body
X4 Silverstone with Cadillac engine
X5 1st Nash Healey (Silverstone) prototype
X6 1st Nash Healey prototype with all enveloping body
X7 Long wheel base (9 ft) Nash Healey
X11 1st J type Healey Hundred: Show car
X12 2nd J type Healey Hundred: chassis only
X14 and X15 1953 Nash Healey race cars
X102 Nash Healey Coupé race car
X114 Special light bodied Nash Healey – 3rd Le Mans 1952
X133 'K' type chassis
X150 1954 – AH 100 prototype
X160 1st 100 S chassis
X170 'L' type chassis
X179 'L2' type chassis
X185 100-Six for Monte Carlo Rally 1958
X191 100 S Show car
X201 'P' type multitube chassis car
X207 6 cylinder prototype NWD 977

X216 2nd 6 cylinder prototype
X220 1st 'Q' type, later Sprite
X221 2nd 'Q' type, later Sprite
X224 car with Ferrari engine
X250 'T' type chassis
X251 De Dion type axle on BN6
X300 3000 prototype
X312 Coupé-bodied 3000 GT
X400 4 litre Rolls-Royce 'R' engined prototype

X numbers were not taken out in date order.

Index

AC Delco safety unit, 167
ADO 24, 171
AHR5–8, 75
AP clutch, 177
Abbey panels, 40
Abecassis, George, 132
Aero parts Engineering, 32–3
Air brakes, 29
Air resistance, 27
Air suspension, 38
Al-Fin brake drums, 79
Alfa Romeo 2900, 30
Alford and Alder,70
Alpine Rally 1949, 40
Alumium panels, 32, 68, 77, 124, 151, 153
Alvis 3 litre engine, 55
American Automobile Association, 91, 93, 112
Appleyard, Ian, 40
Armstrong dampers, 136
Armstrong shock absorber links, 156
Armstrong Siddely Motors, 35, 47, 50, 71
Armstrong Whitworth Aircraft, 51, 103–104
Austin of America, 64
Austin Healey 100, 56, 60–72
Austin Healey 100s, 101–106, 122–45
Austin Healey 175 HP engine, 163
Austin Healey Sprite, 151–63, 181–6
Austin Healey Club of America's conclave, 194
Austin Healey Club Midland Centre, 158

Austin Healey Club Pacific Centre, 194
Austin Healey Club South-Western Centre, 171
Austin Healey Special Test Cars, 74–86
Austin Healey Sports and Touring Club's encounter, 194
Austin Motor Co., 71
   agreement with Donald Healey, 60
   engines, 56
   support for 100S, 126
Auto Transmissions, 68
Automobile Club of Brescia, 44, 100
Automobile Racing Club of Florida, 97
Automobile Review, 81

BN 1, 2 and 4, 71
BRICO, 49–50
Baker, Clive, 179
Barnett, John, 103
Barratt, Mike, 71
Bartlett, Onslow, 40
Bassi, Aldo, 44–5
Becquart, Marcel, 83, 84
Bendix brakes, 53
Benett, John Gordon, 93
Bentley and Bastow, 35
Bentley, W. O., 35
Bilbie, Barry, 61, 75, 88, 89, 162, 177
Birmabright, 37, 77, 177
Blue Hills Mine Hill, 17
Boardman, Bob, 63, 88
Bodywork, 62–3, 146, 151, 153–4
   see also Aluminium panels; Paint

Bonneville Salt Flats, Utah, 86–94,
    110–14, 118–21
Borg and Beck, 78, 107, 130
Borg Warner overdrive, 47, 54, 68
Bowden, Ben, 24, 30
Boyle, Edward, 48
Brabham, Jack, 181
Brakes, 29, 53, 65, 79, 131
    see also Dunlop; Ferodo, Girling
Bramwell and Whitehead, 176
Brandist, Harry, 63, 72
Braunsweig, Robert 81
Bresica Automobile club, 44, 100
British Empire Trophy Race, Isle of
    Man 1951, 53
British Motor Holdings, 137
British Motor Corporation: competi-
    tions department, 124
    formation, 129
    6 cylinder, 137
British Racing Drivers Club production
    car race, Silverstone 1949, 40;
    1951, 53
Brown, David, gearboxes, 96–7, 107,
    129
Buckingham, Bill 177
Bugatti 2300, 30
Bumpers, 79
Bundy tubes, 153
Burman steering gear, 153
Burzi, Dick, 157
Bussey, Ed, 131, 134–5

Cabantous, Ives Giraud, 58–9
Cadillac V8 engine, 41, 44–6
Cam Gears, 173
Camshaft, 133
Cape engineering, 38
Cape Factory, Warwick (The Works),
    64, 87, 151
Carburettors, 41, 48, 106, 133, 154, 190
Carter, Arthur, 136
Cashmore, Jim, 132, 151, 162
Castagneto, Commendatore Renzo, 44

Castrol:
    clutch pump system, 88, 91
    oil, 54, 87
Chambers, marcus, 122, 146
Champion spark plugs, 118, 179
Chiron, Louis, 100, 101
City Street Metal, 56
Clark, Charles, 131
Clayton, Wright, 51
Clegg, Lionel, 134
Clutches, 68, 78
Coker, Gerry, 51, 53, 58, 62–3, 70, 75,
    88, 101, 103, 106, 115, 124–5, 135
Collins, Peter, 161, 162
Columbia quick change axle centre,
    41
Conolly's, 77
Cooper, Geoff, 60, 74, 76
Core plugs, 40
Costley, Harry, 51
Coten End cinema, 151
Coventry Climax V8 engine, 181
Cox, Peter, 171
Crankshafts, 77, 127
Cross, Tony, 176
Cueillier, François, 51
Cunningham, Briggs, 41, 44
Cutler, Mervya, 35
Cylinder:
    block, 12
    heads, 56–8
    number of, 29

DAS 10 shock absorbers, 122, 157
Daltwyler, Willy, 81
Dampers, 27
    see also Suspension
Densham, John, 35
Dockers, 77, 125
Dolby, Ossie, 35
Douglas of Bristol, 70
Draper, Fred, 63, 88
Dryden, Curly, 38
Duncan, Ian, 68

Dunlop:
  brakes, 85, 95, 97, 100–103, 136
  tyres, 34, 36, 88, 92, 108, 111, 133,
    179, 185–6
  wheels, 38, 88, 97, 176
Dutton, Reeves, 112
Dynamos, 127

Edwards, J. R. (Joe), 61, 71
Elektron alloy wheels, 176
Elliot, Samuel, and Sons, 33
Energy, alternative sources, 188–9
Enever, Roger, 181, 186
Enever, Syd, 111, 163
Everflex trim, 77
Eves, Ted, 49
Eyston, G. E. T. (George), 87–8, 91–3,
  106, 114, 118–19

F8, 166
Ferodo NE 99 linings, 83
Ferrari 2.5 litre engine, 161–2
Fins, 106
Fire extinguisher system, 108
Firestone tyres, 190
Fitch, John, 58
Flockhart, Ron, 118, 131, 132
Forbes-Robinson, 135
Ford:
  Fiesta, 190–91
  gearbox, 41, 44
  Mexico engine, 190
Foster, Bernard, 177
Fowler, Cyril, 71, 130
Frames, rigidity, 25–6
Frick adaptor plate, 42, 44
Frick, Bill, 41
Frick Tappet Motors, 41

Gardner, Graham, 71
Gastonides, Maurice, 83
Gayden RAF base, 90, 108, 186

Gearboxes:
  Austin taxis, 77–8, 81
  David Brown, 96–7, 107, 129
  100S, 127, 129–30
General Motors V8 engine, 181
Geneva Motor show: 1953, 80
  1972, 186
Girling brakes, 51, 53, 79, 86, 100–102,
  157, 176, 185
Glass reinforced plastic (GRP) bodies,
  151
Goffin, Jack, 89, 115, 129, 163
Goodall, Morris (Mort), 50, 80, 97,
  100, 114
Goodwood 9 Hour Race 1953, 86
Grant, Gregor, 82–3
Graviner fire fighting equipment, 108
Green, Brian, 71
Green, Doug, 177
Griffin, Charles, 163
Grinham, Ted, 48

Hadley, Bert, 59, 83
Hamilton, Duncan, 50, 54, 55
Harriman, George, 61, 126, 157
Harris, John, 179, 186
Harris, Ken, 71
Harrison, Jimmy, 111, 113
Harrison, Robert, 184
Hassan, Wally, 50, 172, 179
Hawley, Don, 89, 103
Healey Automobile Consultants, 187
Healey, Brian (Bic), 10, 124, 181, 187
Healey, Donald Mitchell (DMH), 12
  autobiography, 13–23
  'The Enthusiast's Car', 25–9
Healey, Donald, Motor Co., 187
Healey family, 11
Healey Fiesta, 190
Healey 'G' type, 55
Healey hundred *see* Austin Healey 100
Healey, Ivy, 10
Healey, John, 10
Healey, Margot, 49, 81
Healey Silverstone *see* X2

Healey 3 litre, 55
Healey 2.4 litre Roadster/Saloon, 30–34, 36
Hedges, Andrew, 179, 186
Hewland DG 300 gearbox, 177
Heynes, Bill, 181
Hiduminium forgings, 32
High Duty Alloys, 32
Hobson, H. M., 63
Hodges, Len, 38–9, 53
Hogg, Tony, 190
Horner, Fred, 91, 110
Hotel du Croissant, Cerams Foulle-torte, 55
Hounslow, Alec, 111
Humphries, Don, 158
Huntoon, George, 97, 135
Hysert, Lysle, 111

International Healey Day, 194
International Motor Show 1952, 60
Invicta 41/2, 30
Ireland, Les, 151
Issigonis, Alec, 163

James Cycle Co., 70
Jenkins, Abe, 87
Jensen, Dick, 124
Jensen Healey, 186–7
Jensen Motors, 64–5, 70, 71, 76–7, 115, 124, 129, 153–4, 157, 187–8
Johnson, Leslie, 56, 58–9
Judd, John, 181

KWD 947, 53
Keall, C. A., 13
Kenny, Tom, 50–51, 53
Kohs, Gary, 153
Koni shock absorber, 190

Ladd, Harry, 71
Land's End–John-O'-Groats trial 1924, 18

Launte, Doug de, 35
Laycock de Normanville, 58, 68, 78, 154
Layrub couplings, 106
Le Mans 24 Hours Race:
  1950, 49–51
  1951, 51, 54–5
  19532, 59, 61, 83
  1955, 133
  1965, 153
  1966, 153
  1967, 153
  1968, 153, 172, 179, 181
  1969, 181–4, 186
Lee, Leonnard, 172, 181
Leland, Bill, 106, 107, 115
Leston, Les, 133
Leyland Australia, 184
Light, Ken, 79
Lockett, Johnny, 83, 86
Lockheed air struts, 38
London–Land's End trial:
  1923, 16
  1924, 17–18
  1925, 18
Lord Len, 56, 60, 74, 76, 87, 90, 129
Low, Jack, 126
Lubrication, piped chassis, 88, 91
Lucas:
  components, 179, 185
  dynamo, 36–7, 127
  lamps, 53
  overdrive switches, 81
  petrol injection, 181
Lurani, Count Johnny, 36
Luvax Bijur, 88
Lyons-Chabonnières Rally 1953, 83

MCC, 18
MG, 171, 194
McKenzie, Bill, 56
McLeods, Clarence, Motel, 91
Macklin, Lance, 97–101, 130–33, 135
Machining, 63
Maggi, Count Aymo, 44

Maher, Eddie, 33, 89, 115, 126, 129, 133, 163
Mann, Nigel, 50
Marshall superchargers, 115
Marston Radiators, 79
Mason, George, 46, 51
Menadue, Roger, 24, 33, 36, 41–2, 48, 50–51, 56, 61, 72, 75–6, 80–82, 86, 88–90, 97, 101, 106, 107, 110, 119, 151, 162
Mercedes, SSK, 30
Mercer, Bertie, 83
Merralls, Jack, 70
Miami World Fair 1953, 71
Michelin tyres, 53
Millard, Peter, 71
Mille Miglia Road Race:
    1948, 36–7
    1949, 49
    1951, 53
    1952, 55–6
    1953, 58, 61, 83
    1954, 100–101
    1955, 131·3
Minilite wheels, 190
Mintex linings, 53, 65, 68, 79, 82
Mintex pads, 129, 157
Moore, Meade F., 46
Moore, Roy Jackson, 114, 119, 135
Morris engines, 115, 127, 129, 130, 163
Morris Motors, 126
Mortimer, Charles, 41
Motor Industry Research Association (MIRA), 35, 58, 179
Motor Trophy 1968, 181
Moss, Stirling, 51, 98, 130–31, 133, 136
Muir, Reg, 72

NH 2023, 51
NOJ 391, 80, 82–6
NOJ 392, 82, 83, 86
NOJ 393, 83, 86, 133
Nash Healey Specials, 47–59
Nash Motors, 46, 126
    Ambassador 1951, 53

cylinder heads, 56–8
engines, 47, 56, 58
Statesman 1950, 53
Nassau races, 162–3
New York International Motor Sports Fair 1953, 71
Nitriding, 77

ONX 113, 102
OON 439, 132
Opus ignition system, 185
Overdrives, 47, 54, 68, 81

Pacific Center's Austin Healey West 194
Paint, 77, 106, 125
Palm Beach, Florida 1950, 40
Panel craft, 51
Panels *see* Aluminium panels
Parnell, Reg, 53
Perry, George, 89
Pinin Farina, 55
Pirelli tyres, 36
Pistons, 127
Plessey hydraulic pumps, 95–6
Plugs *see* Spark plugs
Polley, Ian, 153
Poole, Alec, 181
Portago, Marquis de, 161
power requirements, 27–9
Power units *see* Engines
Pressed Steel, 163
Price, Geoff, 64, 72
Princess R model, 166
Protheroe, Dick, 134
Purchasing, 63

Qvale, Kjell, 187

RB 740/127E, 184
Radiators, 79
Railton, Reid, 30

Rawson, Lionel, 51, 106
Record attempts, 86–94, 110–14
Red Bug *see* X1
Redmayne joint, 176
Reece, Peter, 82
Reid, Jock, 83, 97, 98
Repco Brabham 3 litre Formula One
    engine, 181–2
Richards, Robin, 40
Riley (Coventry) Ltd., 29, 33
    9 Brooklands, 29–30
    2.4 litre engine, 30, 33
Riley, Percy, 30
Riley, Peter, 40
Riley, Victor, 17
Road and Track, 190–91
Rocker shafts, 58
Roesch, Georges, 30
Rolling resistance, 27
Rolls Royce, 77, 166, 167
Rolt, Tony, 40, 50, 53–5
Rover V8 engine, 181, 191
Rubirosa, P., 98
Rudd, Ken, 86
Running in, 80
Ryan, Jack, 71

SPL 224B, 75, 80
SPL 227B, 75, 86, 90, 115
SPL 256, BN, 97
SPL 257 BN, 97
SPL 258 BN, 97
SPL 259 BN, 97, 103
SR, 151, 172–86
ST 224, 225, 226, 227, 74
SU:
    carburettors, 41, 48, 106, 133, 154
    pumps, 89, 107
Safety, 108
Salt corrosion, 115
Salvadori, Roy, 163
Sampietro, A. C. (Sammy), 24, 30, 32,
    38, 49, 53, 57
Sampietro Grand Hotel, Tremezzo, 49

Sandri, Carlo, 36
Saxton, John (Sacco), 51
Sayer, Malcolm, 181
Scott Brown, Archie, 135
Seats, 53, 77, 125, 156–7
Sebring 12 Hour Grand Prix of Endur-
    ance:
    1954, 97–9
    1955, 129
    1956, 135
    1965, 153
    1966, 153
    1967, 153
    1968, 153
Serafini, Dorino, 36
Shelby, Carroll, 114, 119, 121
Sharp, Mike, 134
Ship and Shore, 131
Shock absorbers, 27, 71, 122, 157, 190,
    see also Suspension
Shorrock, Noel and Chris, 106
Sigrist, Freddy, 15
Silverstone:
    production car race 1949, 40; 1951, 53
    tests at, 179
Silverstone *see* X2
Simpson, Peter, 40
Smith, Reggie, 97
Smiths instrumentation, 177
Soans, C. H., and Sons, 44
Society of Motor Manufacturers and
    Traders, 60
Sopwith Aviation Co., 15
Spark plugs, 108, 118, 179
Spear, Bill, 93
Spears, Harry, 172
Speed of the Wind, 87–8
Speed records *see* Record attempts
Spoilers, 29
Sport cars definition, 25
Springing, 26–7
Standard motors, 48–9
Stansbury, Ken, 35, 47, 50
Steering geometry, 26, 162
Stokes, Lord, 181
Streamlining, 28

Stroke/bore ratio, 29
Styles, Phil, 135
Styling, 63, 124
Superchargers, 106, 115, 118
Superflexit oil hoses, 130
Suspension, 26, 38, 173 *see also* Dampers; Shock absorbers

Talbot 95, 30
Targa Florio 1948, 36
Taylor, Ken, 57–8
Thompson, Jimmy, 126
Thompson, John, 47, 77, 124, 172
Thompson and Taylor, 57
Thornhill. Peter, 38, 51
Thorpe, Doug, 153
Timkin bearings, 83
Tour de France, 53, 86
Towermaster lattice tower, 189
Transmission, 29
Trengwainton Bank Holiday Hill Climb
    1949, 45
Triumph TR Series, 136–7
Truro and District Motor Club, 16
Turbochargers, 115, 118
Turner, Gerry, 38
Tyres, 34
    see also Dunlop; Firestone; Michelin;
    Pirelli

UOC 741, 146
Ulmann, Alec, 97

Vale, Eric, 71
Valves, 127
Vandervell crankshaft, 127
Veyron, Pierre, 58, 59
Volpati, Dr., 38

Wakefield, C. C., Ltd., 87
Walter, Phil, 41
Wardle, Bernard, 77
Water-leaks, 71, 82
Weaving, John (doc), 106, 107, 115, 120
Weber carburettors, 190
Weslake, Harry, 89, 98, 99, 126
Westland Motor Co., 32
Westwood, Derek, 177
Westwood, Terry, 151, 177
Wheel location, 26
Wheels, 38, 88, 97, 176
Wilkes, Peter, 181
Wilks, Peter, 156
Willday, Ray, 58
Wilkins, Gordon, 83, 84
Williams, George, 118
Wilmott Breedon, 79
Wimby, Cecil, 49–50
Winby, Cecil, 86
Wind tunnels, 103, 106
Windmills, as alternative energy
    sources, 188–9
Wisdom, Tommy, 58, 100, 101, 146
Wodsworth, Edgar, 40
Wondarweld, 119
Wood, George, 79
Wood, Ray, 179, 186
Woods, Andy, 71
Wright, Joe, 96

X1 (Red Bug), 38
X2 (Healey Silverstone), 40–45, 47
X4, 41, 45
X5, 48–9, 51, 53, 56, 58
X8, 56, 58
X14, 58
X15, 58
X224, 162–3
X312, 153
XR37, 151, 172–86